ICELANDIC
FOLKTALES
& LEGENDS

ICELANDIC FOLKTALES & LEGENDS

JACQUELINE SIMPSON

TEMPUS

First published 1972
This edition first published 2004
Reprinted 2006

Tempus Publishing Limited
The Mill, Brimscombe Port,
Stroud, Gloucestershire, GL5 2QG
www.tempus-publishing.com

British Library Cataloguing in Publication Data.
A catalogue record for this book is available from the British Library.

ISBN 0 7524 3045 9

Typesetting and origination by Tempus Publishing Limited
Printed and bound in Great Britain

CONTENTS

FOREWORD

What a pleasure it is to welcome this re-issue of Jacqueline Simpson's classic collection of *Icelandic Folktales and Legends*! It's a book I practically grew up with; that's a bit of an exaggeration, I admit, as it is only 30 years or so since it was first published, but it *seems* as if I have had it on my shelves forever. As an Icelander, I was brought up on these folktales from childhood, in the original Icelandic; yet Jacqueline Simpson's translations are so vivid, so clear, so delightfully fresh, that they feel seamlessly original in their own right.

Dr Simpson had already presented an anthology of translated excerpts and tales from the Icelandic sagas and eddas (*The Northmen Talk*, 1965) which were models of simple clarity and accuracy. Her 'conversion' to Icelandic folktales was a marvellous stroke of good luck. Not only did it set her on the path to becoming Britain's most eminent academic folklorist, with a host of publications on British and Scandinavian folklore – it rescued from near oblivion a treasure trove of northern tales of trolls and giants and ghosts and elves which were all but unknown to the English-speaking world. Some are scary, some are touching, some are downright funny – all of them are memorable.

Icelandic trolls were giant-sized; they live on in the grotesque shapes left by cooling lava, which were interpreted as trolls who had been turned to stone when they were caught by the rising sun. Most of the stories about them feature lascivious, metaphorically man-eating ogresses – a standard motif. But there were nice trolls, too: and the tale of 'Bergthor of Blafell' is an enchanting example – especially because, just outside the churchyard at Haukadalur, there is an outsize grave said to be the friendly neighbourhood giant's last resting place.

The sense of place is so important in these tales. So is the identification with real people. Icelandic ghosts were real people who, after death, became revenants intent on harming the living. The story of 'The Deacon of Myrka' is not only a chilling ghost story – it also casts a chill on the farms in the area to this day.

My own favourites concern the elves, known in Iceland as *huldu-folk* – the 'Hidden Folk'. Many Icelanders still believe in them – more or less. Icelandic elves are for the most part invisible, but otherwise they are just like humans and live like humans. But they are idealised humans – the wish-fulfilments of a poverty-stricken people. They live in communities, especially in hillocks or boulders, and these homesteads have been considered sacrosanct for centuries. Indeed, there are several instances in modern Iceland of road-building projects being redesigned in order to avoid dynamiting a boulder or demolishing a hillock which was said to be the domicile of elves. No, don't laugh – it's true.

Perhaps the most enchanting of the tales in this book is the very first one: 'The Origin of Elves'. That, to me, is where folk-fable ultimately merges into the profound reality of folk-truth.

This is such a lovely book. Welcome back! I positively purr whenever I open it.

Magnus Magnusson

PREFACE

The titles I have given to individual stories are not always direct translations of their Icelandic names, though in many cases they are; the original names, where these differ, are given in the notes. Icelandic proper names are anglicised in the text, but given in their Icelandic form in the notes and introduction. Explanation of the abbreviations and references used in the notes can be found on pp.217–19. An Index of Tale Types appears on pp.220–1.

I am grateful to Benedikt Benedikz for his generous help on points of translation and interpretation; he is of course not responsible for whatever errors remain.

Worthing October 1971
Jacqueline Simpson

INTRODUCTION

The folk legends of Iceland are too little known outside the borders of their own land, particularly in England. This is equally true whether one compares their readership with that of medieval Icelandic sagas and poetry, frequently translated and much studied in Britain, or with that of the folktales of other European countries, say Ireland or France or even Norway – let alone those of Germany, now for several generations adopted as part of the British heritage, thanks to a constant flow of translations from the work of the Brothers Grimm. In contrast, Jón Árnason's two large volumes of *Íslenzkar fijó ϗsögur og Aefintýri*, ('The Folktales and Fairy Tales of Iceland'), 1862–4, one of the major products of the great nineteenth-century period of folktale collecting, have received only rare and partial renderings into English; moreover, the selected translations by G.E.J. Powell and Eiríkur Magnússon in 1864 and 1866, the only ones that can claim to offer a representative range of material, are stylistically most unsatisfactory, being full of repetitiveness, circumlocutions and pomposity.

The present work too is only a selection, taken chiefly from Jón Árnason's first three chapters, those on supernatural beings, ghosts and magic. I have thought it better to give a fairly thorough coverage to a few topics rather than to skim the surface of the whole work; among the subjects I have left untouched are the cycle of legends about Master Magicians, those about outlaws, those about seers and others with psychic powers, numskull stories, and the *Märchen*, i.e. fairy tales in the popular sense of the term. The topics chosen here are all such as to provide opportunity not only for the study of Icelandic folk-beliefs but also for comparison with similar material in other cultures, including our own.

Jón Árnason (1819–88) and his friend the Revd Magnús Grímsson (1825–60) were stimulated by their admiration for the work of the Grimms and by the growth of folklore studies in Europe to undertake the collecting of traditional tales, beliefs, and verses in their own land. They were both too poor to spare time or money roaming the countryside as collectors; Jón Árnason was librarian of what later became the National Library of Reykjavík, and eked out a meagre salary with teaching and secretarial work; Magnús Grímsson was a schoolmaster, later a clergyman, besides writing poetry, plays, novels and translations. However, both men had contacts all over Iceland, principally with their own former pupils who had become teachers and clergymen, and it was very largely in the form of written accounts by these men that the material was gathered in.

When and how the collaboration between Jón Árnason and Magnús Grímsson began is uncertain; as early as 1845 the latter was collecting directly from his young pupils (tales marked in the notes as being 'from a schoolboy from X, 1845' belong to this early phase of the work). In 1852 they published a few samples of their already considerable material as a small book, *Íslenzk Aefintýri*. But during the next few years their activity slackened, since there seemed little hope of publishing more, until in 1858 they were encouraged by the enthusiasm of a visiting German scholar, Konrad Maurer, who toured Iceland for six months gathering material for his *Isländische Volkssagen der Gegenwart* (1860). He urged them to resume their work, and suggested the possibility of publication in Leipzig. By this stage, however, Magnús Grímsson was taking less part in the task, and towards the end of 1860 he died. Jón Árnason continued alone; he wrote to all his correspondents, urging them to send in whatever they had found, and flung himself into the task of comparing, selecting and organising the vast mass that had accumulated. The book eventually appeared in two parts, being printed in Leipzig in 1862 and 1864; numerous manuscripts containing unused variants were later deposited in the National Library at Reykjavík. Much of this material has now been published in the enlarged third edition of his book, in six volumes (Reykjavík, 1954–61), which also contains notes and indexes.

These tales (like those of other lands) can be roughly classified into two major groups: the 'folk legends' (Icelandic þjóðsagnir, German *Sagen*), which are believed to be true by teller and hearers alike, and are generally attached to real places and persons; and the 'Wonder Tales' or 'Fairy Tales' (Icelandic *aefintýri*, German *Märchen*), told as entertaining fantasies. There are also other minor types, such as pious tales and jocular tales. The stories in Jón Árnason's first volume belong to the first group, as do most of those in the present selection. Of course, in practice there are many gradations of belief: ghost stories are normally taken very seriously indeed, but 'The Boy who Knew no Fear' is almost pure buffoonery; the she-troll is often a figure of fun, as in 'How Kraka Lost her Lover', but the murderous troll who severs fowlers' ropes was still dreaded on Grimsey in the middle of the nineteenth century (see 'Blessing the Cliffs'); the belief in changelings was firmly rooted, but there is a lighter tone about 'Father of Eighteen Elves' than about 'The Changeling who Stretched'; parents taught their children to fear the bugbear Grýla, but did not believe in her themselves.

Owing to the number of sagas and other literary works surviving from medieval Iceland, many of them incorporating elements drawn from contemporary folktales and beliefs, one can often trace the existence of various stories, motifs and beliefs back to the twelfth, thirteenth and fourteenth centuries, or in some cases even to the poems and myths of heathen times. This aspect of Icelandic folktales has been systematically covered by Einar Ól. Sveinsson in two books, *Verzeichnis Isländischer Märchenvarienten*, Helsinki 1929, and *Um Íslenzkar þjóðsögur*, Reykjavík 1940. The latter has now been revised and translated into English by B.S. Benedikz under the title *The Folk-Stories of Iceland* (London, 2003). It now includes (pp. 141–8) an updated list of collections of Icelandic folk-stories and folklore, and studies thereof (almost all in Icelandic). In my notes to individual tales, I have mentioned the earliest known occurrences in Iceland of particular story-types, where these are significantly earlier than Jón Árnason's examples. But I have made no attempt to pursue their later history by giving parallels from collections made after Jón Árnason's time.

As a glance at the Index of Tale Types (pp. 220–1) will show, there are many affinities between these stories and the general corpus of European folktales. This is true both of *Märchen*, numbered according to the international classification of Antti Aarne and Stith Thompson (indicated by the letters AT), and of many local and historical *Sagen*, called 'Migratory Legends' by the Norwegian scholar Reidar Th. Christiansen, and here numbered according to his system (indicated by the letters ML). The pursuit of international parallels could lead far afield; I have in the main confined myself to the other Scandinavian lands, as having the closest links with Iceland, and to a few instances of comparable material from the British Isles.

Despite their foreign parallels, these Icelandic stories are almost always very firmly localised. They often have a strong aetiological element: this specified rock or island is a giant turned to stone; that hollow in the ground, the site of a sunken church; a church door-ring, a horse-block, a vestment, or an altar-cloth, has some legend to account for its existence, and is in turn regarded as proof of the legend. Other types of story are explanatory in a broader sense, 'explaining' calamities, whether individual or communal: lost children have been kidnapped by elves, sickly children and mental defectives are changelings; the persistent illness or bad luck of a family is the work of a ghost that 'follows' it from generation to generation; recurrent fatal accidents on a particular cliff are due to a troll inside it.

Often one can see how personal experiences (usually grim ones) are interpreted in terms of a pre-existent belief, which they then serve to reinforce. This is very clear in some ghost stories, where nightmares and obsessional guilts and fears loom large (e.g. 'Mother Mine, Don't Weep', 'The Lovers', or 'Thorgeir's Bull'). In a similar way, one can see a sick woman's hallucination in 'The Changeling who Stretched', and a child's dream or fantasy in 'Dr Skapti Sæmundsson' and 'Making a Changeling'. The fear instilled by mountain solitudes is reflected in some of the troll tales; one may even wonder whether 'Trunt, Trunt and the Trolls in the Fells' can have been based on observation of some half-crazed man who took to a solitary life in the wilds, and there degenerated year by year.

More cheerful motifs are not lacking. Many reflect the normal wishes and dreams of a hard-working and often poverty-ridden community: wealth may be given by elves, taken by force from ghosts, or found in a 'money tussock' or a haunted mound; marvellous cows may appear from the sea or the elves' herds; one may be given knowledge, medical skill, or farming and fishing luck by elves, or simply a fine helping of porridge by a good-natured troll. There is much humour in the stories, too. Sometimes it flickers grimly round macabre topics, as in 'How Petur Got his Wall-Eye' and 'The Priest and the Farmer', but more often it is purely comic: the frustrated she-troll in hot pursuit of her reluctant lover, brandishing the allegedly aphrodisiac shark; the sardonic merman, proffering double-edged wisdom; the stock 'old man' and 'old woman' whose stupidity, obstinacy or shrewdness are the theme of many anecdotes. A strain of gentle pathos runs through other tales, telling of tragic love between elves and human girls, represented here by 'The Girl at the Shieling'; several sixteenth-century poems were written round such themes, and though their pathos may come too close to sentimentality for modern tastes, they were long popular, and have a charm of their own.

A comparison between the supernatural beings of Icelandic and British lore presents many points of interest. The elves, more commonly called the 'Hidden People', correspond to British fairies, and many of the same stories are told of them. They differ, however, in being always of full human size, and indeed only distinguishable from human beings by some tiny detail – a ridge instead of a groove in the upper lip, or the absence of any division between the nostrils. Their social organisation is visualised in considerable detail as a reflection, sometimes idealised, of human society; they live in communities in hillocks, inside mountains, or in invisible farm-steads; they live by farming and fishing (but do not have a specialised characteristic activity, as the leprechaun does); they go to market, hold religious services, and are sometimes said to have a king.

The attitude towards them revealed in the tales and beliefs is ambiguous. Sometimes they are dreaded as child-stealers, as the bringers of sickness, as cruel, revengeful, or wantonly malignant; sometimes, on the contrary, they are said to reward goodness and courage, to punish only the undeserving, and to help and protect their human friends. In some stories they are heathen, fearing the name of God or the Cross; in others, they have a religion of their own, with priests, services, sacraments and hymns, all closely modelled on Christianity. This last point is comparatively rare, but not unknown, in British lore; but the other conflicting aspects are common here. It is also worth noting that one common type of British fairy, the individual Brownie who attaches himself to a house to help its owners in their work, is not to be found in Iceland; interestingly, the unpleasant Icelandic 'family ghosts' some-times play poltergeist tricks, as the less agreeable Brownies are said to do, and sometimes have food and a bed set out for them (see 'Mori of Irafell'). As Brownies are sometimes said to be ghosts, the resemblance is probably no accident.

The belief in elves can be traced back to pagan Scandinavian mythology; some of the stories about them which later become common as folktales make their first appearance in medieval sagas, usually in a truncated or distorted form – for instance, that of a human being acting as midwife to a fairy woman. Sixteenth-century writers often show knowledge of elf-lore, and after about 1600 the mention of elves becomes frequent; belief in their actual existence was very strong, and even in the early nineteenth century Ólafur Sveinsson of Purkey collected stories of men's encounters with the Hidden People with as much conviction as the Scottish minister Robert Kirk, who wrote *The Secret Commonwealth* in 1691.

In present-day Iceland, a living belief in elves is still a factor to be reckoned with. It is quite common for the construction of new roads and buildings to be interrupted because a succession of accidents to workmen or their machinery is taken to mean that elves are angry at the disturbance to their own homes or routes; if they are allowed time to move away from the area, or if (better still) the construction plans are changed to avoid damaging the elf homes, work can safely resume. Valdimar Hafstein, who has studied this current lore, notes that elves no longer look and dress just like their human contemporaries; on the contrary, they wear old-fashioned clothes, and tend their cattle and sheep in old-fashioned ways. They now stand for the traditional rural life of Iceland's past, rejecting modern urbanisation.

Icelandic trolls are in most ways the direct descendants of the stupid, dangerous giants of Scandinavian myth, but differ from them in being generally solitary creatures, and in being so often associated with particular rocks and other landmarks. In Iceland, the word 'troll' always denotes a giant, never the little gnomes or elf-like creatures known by that name in Denmark, the Faroes and some regions of Sweden. A few trolls are kindly, but most are bad; most hate Christianity and have no religion of their own, though they are true to their promises. They are quite often presented in a ridiculous light; according to Einar Ól. Sveinsson, the serious belief in their existence was probably dead by 1600 (though among fowlers it may have lingered longer – see 'Blessing the Cliffs'). Tales about them are often intended to explain curious rock formations. Generally these are said to be the troll himself, turned to stone;

occasionally a rock is said to have been thrown by a giant at a church, though this is a less common motif in Iceland than in Norway. Two widespread English notions, that rocks had been thrown by giants at one another or dropped by one engaged on some huge building task, do not appear in Iceland. Probably such legends flourish best where isolated rocks inexplicably crop up in the middle of level land, not where the whole landscape is dominated by rocky masses.

From heathen times onwards, the belief in ghosts has been strongly held in Iceland, and is characterised by the very markedly physical nature of the revenants described. Indeed, the word 'ghost' is hardly a correct rendering of *draugur*, the oldest and commonest term, since this normally refers to an actual corpse emerging from its grave. As in medieval sagas, so also in folktales, the *draugur* is often to be overcome by wrestling, decapitation, or burning; other methods, not mentioned in sagas but equally physical, are piercing the feet with nails, driving a stake through the grave, or covering it with a massive rock. But besides the *draugur* there developed a belief in a more wraith-like type of ghost, the *svipa* or *vofa*, here rendered 'spectre', and in more spiritual or magical means of ghost-laying, such as prayers and Christian rites, or poetic charms and incantations. The type of ghost called a 'Sending', i.e. one called up by a wizard and working at his command, is non-material in its mode of action (e.g. it is often invisible, or it takes on various shapes at will), but is held to originate in a corpse, or at least a bone or other part of a body, whether human or animal, into which the wizard has 'put strength'. There are some interesting similarities and differences between the reasons given in Icelandic and in British lore for the activities of ghosts. Both lands have 'family ghosts', but where the British type is often quite harmless, the *fylgidraugur* (who is often a hostile Sending) persecutes those whom he 'follows' with illnesses and misfortunes for many generations, and attacks people in the neighbourhood as well. Both have vindictive ghosts, resenting wrongs suffered in life, or disrespect to their bones in death, but Icelandic ghosts do not often denounce ancient crimes (although ghosts of infants do haunt their guilty mothers). Both have misers' ghosts, but whereas the British type is restless and conscience-stricken, longing only to make amends by revealing his hoard, the Icelandic *fépúki* usually gloats grotesquely over his wealth, which can only be got from him by trickery or force. Indeed, remorseful ghosts, so common elsewhere, are comparatively rare in Iceland; even the international tale of 'The Unforgiven Dead' is there handled more in terms of a feud between two of the dead than as a matter of moral guilt and pardon (see 'The Woman in the Red Cap').

Ghost lore in Iceland is closely linked to magic lore, with much stress on methods of raising and laying ghosts and making use of them for one's own purposes. For though many walk for reasons of their own, many others are called up by some necromancer who masters them and 'sends' them against his enemies. To some extent, this grim notion is foreshadowed in early mythological texts alluding to the necromantic arts of Óðinn, but there the stress is on occult wisdom and powers of prophecy, not on harmful sorcery; the full series of beliefs concerning Sendings and the raising of the dead only became really prominent in the seventeenth and eighteenth centuries, as part of a whole complex of beliefs in sorcery and spells which swept over Icelandic society at that period, causing deep fear and many accusations of witchcraft.

This upsurge of magical beliefs was certainly in part a reflection of the witch-hunting mania that had reached its peak in Europe somewhat earlier, and of the widespread contemporary interest in occult lore among learned men. In Iceland, as elsewhere, books of spells, magic symbols, rituals, and so forth, circulated in considerable numbers, in manuscript form. But the theories of the learned Continental witch-hunters did not take root as deeply in Icelandic folk-belief as elsewhere; for instance, the notion of the Sabbath to which witches fly by night, of the pact with Satan, and of devil-worship, are hardly ever found in Icelandic folktales (cf. notes to 'Hild, Queen of the Elves' and 'The Witch Bridle' below), nor are they prominent in actual trials there.

The black magic of Iceland often gives an even more archaic impression than the evidence of rural fears and practices brought forward in British trials, let alone the bookish theories and the Continental 'confessions' based on them – but that is not to say that Icelandic magic is less gruesome, especially in its pre-occupation with corpses and bones. The milk-stealing 'Carrier', for example, made by the witch herself from a human rib, seems a more primitive notion than the familiar or imp given to the witch by the devil in British lore, even though the 'Carrier' is first mentioned in the seventeenth century. Similarly, the idea of a 'Sending' in the form of a fly or a flayed bull appears first around the same period, but might well be much older; the procedure by which a would-be seer captures a 'Speaking Spirit' has a very archaic, shamanistic air; and the ritual of 'sitting out' is undoubtedly old, though its aim changed in later centuries from obtaining occult knowledge to winning elfin treasures.

It would be wrong to omit all mention of white magic in Icelandic folk-belief, even though it plays less part than sorcery in the stories chosen for inclusion here. From the earliest times, Icelandic sagas take for granted the existence of 'natural' psychic gifts in certain individuals, in particular second sight (both precognition and the power to 'see' invisible beings and distant events), and the ability to read omens and to 'dream true'. Such powers are very often credited to seers and white magicians in later folktales, together with the authority and techniques required to lay ghosts, counteract spells, rescue persons carried off by fairies, kill vermin by the power of a verse, and so forth. Belief in the magic force of a well-turned rhyme goes back to the Middle Ages, and tales about a *kraptaskáld*, 'Poet of Might', are common from the sixteenth to the nineteenth century. Priests in particular were very frequently thought to have magical or other supernatural powers, and there are many traditional tales told about such men who came to be considered as 'Master Magicians', whether of white, grey or black magic. Some of these legends (which form an extensive and important cycle) can be found in my *Legends of Icelandic Magicians*

(Cambridge and Totowa NJ, 1975), with an introduction by B.S. Benedikz which discusses the genre as a whole (previously printed in *Durham University Journal* in 1964).

As has been already remarked, Jón Árnason's collection was not taken verbatim from folk storytellers, but from written versions sent in by teachers, priests and other educated men who acted as his collectors, and concerning whose methods of fieldwork we know little. It is these men whose names generally appear in the notes; attributions to 'a schoolboy from X' or 'an old woman from Y' are less frequent. Only occasionally does one catch what must be the individual voice of one of the primary narrators (one of the schoolboys, for example, has a liking for the phrase 'increase and multiply and fill the earth', and uses it as equivalent to 'live happily ever after'). The possibility that the texts have been touched up cannot be ruled out – indeed, literal fidelity to the spoken tale was an ideal hardly envisaged by most nineteenth-century folklorists.

However, any editorial intervention there may have been in Jón Árnason's texts is by no means the stylistic calamity which it would most likely have been in England in the 1860s. Iceland was more unified in class and culture than other countries; a high proportion of the population was literate, in spite of poverty and hardship; the language had not greatly changed since the Middle Ages; and, above all, the medieval sagas offered a widely-known and admired model for prose narrative style – a style which harmonises admirably with all that is most vigorous, direct and swift-moving in oral storytelling. This harmony is no accident; the sagas themselves, though literary works, sprang from a culture where oral storytelling flourished, and were influenced by its techniques.

In later centuries these sagas were cherished as the products of the golden age of Iceland, and their style was admired as an ideal of 'classic' prose; Jón Árnason's band of collectors, educated men, but reared in this tradition, would have had a far readier appreciation of the oral styles they were likely to encounter than their English contemporaries, trained to admire Latinate diction and complex sentence structures. From sagas, they would be familiar with such features of oral style as abrupt shifts from past to present tense or from reported to direct speech, simplicity in clause and sentence structure, economy of adjectives and adverbs, and a general preference for concision and even dryness over elaboration and emotional explicitness. The gulf between what the primary narrator would consider a good tale well told and what the collector-editor would think acceptable in print was probably narrower in Iceland than anywhere else in mid-nineteenth-century Europe, and consequently any editorial intervention there may have been remains very unobtrusive. In fact, Jón Árnason's own modifications are known to have been, in general, quite slight, and always directed towards simplicity and 'classical' restraint. Often they consisted merely of noting variant details taken from another version of the tale, and are then signalled by some such phrase as 'other people say' – a feature which is itself derived from saga style.

It is probable that knowledge of the sagas helped to form the style of the folktale narrators themselves, though the full extent of the influence could only be assessed by a detailed study of field-recordings. But even among Jón Árnason's texts one can easily see that some tales show more elaboration than others (particularly those that are more *Märchen* than *Sagen*), and that in these cases it is often medieval sagas that provide the model. Examples are 'Bergthor of Blafell', with its typical saga opening, 'There was a man named Bergthor, who lived in a cave on Blafell' (even though the 'man' in question is a troll), and its cross-references to characters in actual sagas; the thumbnail character sketches at the beginning of 'The Boy who Knew no Fear' and 'Hild, Queen of the Elves'; the slow pace and love of picturesque detail in the latter tale, which, though alien to the classic saga style, was a feature of certain more romanticised sagas highly popular in and after the fourteenth century.

One particularly well-loved work, the late thirteenth-century *Grettis saga*, has left its mark on the actual content of several tales: the hiring of the bold shepherd to work on a haunted farm in 'Hild, Queen of the Elves', the wrestling trick which (rather implausibly) floors the ghost in 'The Boy who Knew no Fear', and the eerie effect of moonlight and scudding cloud at the climax of 'The Deacon of Myrka', are all derived from the most famous episode in that saga, the fight between Grettir and the dead Glámr. This last instance is perhaps a trifle suspect; it involves only two sentences, and might therefore be a conscious 'improvement' by the collector, inspired by the reference to moonlight in the verse which is undoubtedly an integral part of the tale. The two others, however, are whole episodes, and occur in stories where the saga influence is very pervasive; they must reflect the story-teller's taste, not just the collector's. The widespread knowledge of the older literature at all levels of Icelandic society easily accounts for these and other instances.

NOTE ON THE SECOND EDITION, 2004

Over the past thirty years, folklorists have paid more attention to the previously neglected genre of the local legend, and far more material has been made available in English for readers interested in its international ramifications. Translations of Scandinavian texts can be found, with commentaries, in Reidar Th. Christiansen, *The Folktales of Norway* (London, 1964); John Lindow, *Swedish Legends and Folktales* (Berkeley and London, 1978); Jacqueline Simpson, *Legends of Icelandic Magicians* (Cambridge and Totowa N.J., 1975); John F. West, *Faroese Folktales and Legends* (Lerwick, 1980); Reimund Kvideland and Henning K. Sehmsdorf, *Scandianvian Folk Belief and Legend* (Minneapolis and Oxford, 1988); Jacqueline Simpson, *Scandinavian Folktales,* (London, 1988). Also worth noting are the chapters on Icelandic world view, magic and the supernatural in Kirsten Hastrup's two books, *Culture and History in Medieval Iceland* (Oxford, 1985), 136–54, and *Nature and Policy in Medieval Iceland* (Oxford, 1990), 245–72.

The modern scholarly apparatus in these works makes them preferable to the older collections of Benjamin Thorpe, *Northern Mythology* (London, 1851, reprint Ware 2001), G.E.J. Powell and Eiríkur Magnússon (*Icelandic Legends*, London 1864), and William

Craigie (*Icelandic Folklore*, London, 1896). Nevertheless, the actual legend texts in the old collections retain their interest; Thorpe's book contains material from parts of Germany, Belgium and the Netherlands as well as Norway, Sweden and Denmark.

Particularly useful for the study of German parallels is Donald Ward's translation of *The German Legends of the Brothers Grimm* (two volumes, London, 1981), which has thorough explanatory and comparative notes upon all the legend types included. (This work, *Deutsche Sagen*, is not to be confused with the more famous *Grimms' Fairy Tales*, i.e. their *Kinder– und Hausmärchen*.) An older collection presenting Scandinavian legends alongside those from parts of Germany and the Netherlands will be found in Benjamin Thorpe's *Northern Mythology* (London, 1851; reprinted, London, 2001).

Irish folklorists too have given increasing attention to their legends, and are examining parallels (and possible links) between these and Nordic material. Papers on the topic will be found in Pádraig Ó Héalaí (ed.), *The Fairy Hill is on Fire!* (= *Béaloideas* 59, Dublin 1991); Pádraig Ó Héalaí (ed.), *Glórtha ón Osnádúr: Sounds from the Supernatural* (= *Béaloideas* 62–3, Dublin 1995); Patricia Lysaght, Séamas Ó Catháin, and D. Ó hÓgain (eds), *Islanders and Water-Dwellers* (Blackrock, 1999); Séamas Ó Catháin (ed.), *Northern Lights* (Dublin, 2001).

The largest single collection of British material is still Katharine Briggs' *Dictionary of British Folk-Tales in the English Language: Part B, Folk Legends* (1971); it reprints or summarises texts from all the major folklore books preceding it. It is thematically arranged, giving a good impression of the range and typical contents of the corpus, and I have therefore used it as the most convenient source of references to Britain in the present work. It should now be supplemented by Jennifer Westwood's *Albion* (1985), where the stories are fewer but their early versions are fully and accurately quoted, and the commentaries are very informative. The past three decades have also seen publication of a number of substantial books on the folklore of some particular county or region, any of which is likely to include some legends not to be found in Briggs. An extensive collection of English local legends by Jennifer Westwood and Jacqueline Simpson is currently (2004) in preparation.

For Scotland, besides general folklore works, there exist two very helpful specialised catalogues of legend types, mainly those found in the Gaelic-speaking areas: Alan Bruford, 'Scottish Gaelic Witch Stories: A Provisional Type-List', *Scottish Studies* 11 (1967), 13–47; Donald Archie MacDonald, 'Migratory Legends of the Supernatural in Scotland: A General Survey', in Pádraig Ó Héalaí (ed.), *Glórtha ón Osnádúr: Sounds from the Supernatural* (= *Béaloideas* 62–3, Dublin 1995), 29–78.

A further large collection of Icelandic folktales and legends (in Icelandic) has appeared: Sigfús Sigfússon, *Íslenszkar fljóˣsögur og sagnir* (11 vols., Reykjavík, 1982–93).

Finally, I would like to thank Dr Terry Gunnell for drawing my attention to many recent articles in Scandinavian journals which are mentioned in the notes to individual stories here, and in the bibliography.

1

THE HIDDEN PEOPLE

THE ORIGIN OF ELVES (I)

Once, God Almighty came to Adam and Eve. They welcomed Him gladly and showed Him everything they had in their house, and they also showed Him their children, who all seemed to Him to be very promising. He asked Eve whether she had any other children besides the ones she was just showing Him. She said 'No.' But the truth of the matter was that Eve had not yet got around to washing some of her children, and so she was ashamed to let God see them, and she had pushed them away somewhere out of sight. God knew this, and said: 'That which had to be hidden from Me, shall also be hidden from men.'

So now these children became invisible to men, and lived in woods and moorlands, knolls and rocks. From them the elves are descended, but human beings are descended from those of Eve's children whom she did show to God. Human beings can never see elves unless the latter wish it, but elves can see men and enable men to see them. It is for this reason that the elves are also called the Hidden People.

J.Á. I 5 (*Huldumannagenesis*); current in many parts of Iceland. This tale, though international, is particularly relevant in Iceland, where the commonest name for elves is *huldufolk*, 'Hidden People' (singular, *hulduma>ur, -kona*, 'Hidden Man, Woman'). These terms, first recorded in the fourteenth century, were thought more polite, and hence safer, than *álfur*, 'elf'. The same story about Eve's children was known elsewhere in

Europe as an explanation of social or ethnic differences (AT 758, 'The Various Children of Eve'). With regard to elves, the story implies that despite differences they are akin to men; the kinship is very clear in Iceland, where they are thought of as barely distinguishable from human beings in appearance, and as having homes, social relationships, and often a religion closely mirroring the human pattern.

For recent discussions of Icelandic elf-lore, see Jón Hnefill A>alsteinsson, 'The Testimony of Waking Consciousness and Dreams in Migratory Legends Concerning Human Encounters with the Hidden People', *Arv* 49 (1993), 123–131; Valdimar Hafstein, 'The Elves' Point of View: Cultural Identity in Contemporary Icelandic Elf Tradition', *Fabula* (2000), 87–104.

THE ORIGIN OF ELVES (II)

O nce, there was a traveller who lost his way and did not know where he was going. At last he came to a farm which he did not recognise at all; there he knocked, and a mature woman came to the door and asked him in, which he accepted. All the furnishings of this farm were excellent. The woman led him into the main room, where two pretty young girls were sitting, but he saw no one else on the farm except for this woman and the two girls. He was welcomed courteously, given food and drink, and later shown to a bed. The man asked if he might sleep with one of the girls, and was told that he could. They lay down together and the man wanted to turn towards her, but he could feel no body where the girl was. He caught hold of her, but there was nothing between his arms, though all the while she lay quietly beside him and he could see her perfectly well. So then he asks her the reason for this.

She says he need not be surprised at it, 'for I am a spirit with no body', says she. 'Long ago, when the Devil raised a revolt in Heaven, he and all who fought for him were driven into outer darkness. But those who were neither for him nor against him and would join neither army were driven down to Earth, and it was decreed that they should live in knolls, hills, and rocks, and they are called elves, or Hidden People. They cannot live with other people, only on their own. They can do both good and evil, and both in the highest degree. They have no bodies such as you humans have, yet they can show themselves to you when they wish. I am one of this band of fallen spirits, so it is not surprising that you cannot get pleasure from me.'

The man had to rest content with that, and later he told the story of what had happened to him.

J.Á. I 5–6, from Jóhannes Jónsson Lund (b. 1804). The theory that elves are a morally intermediate type of spirit between angels and devils is, like the preceding theory, known in many parts of Europe including the British Isles (Briggs 1967, 141, 143–4, 147; Briggs 1978, 30–1). That they should be incapable of sexual intercourse with men is a piece of learned clerical theorising, which is quite counter to the general trend of Icelandic beliefs (cf. pp. 49–56).

THE ELFIN FISHERMAN

It is said that in the old days a farmer lived at Gotur in Myrdal, and that in the fishing seasons he used to row out to what were then and are now the usual fishing grounds for that district, off Dyrhola Isle. One day, as so often, this farmer was coming back from the shore; one has to cross some boggy land, and there, in the half light, he comes upon a man whose horse has fallen in the bog and who cannot get it out unaided. The farmer does not recognise the man, but all the same he helps him to pull the horse out. When the job is done, the unknown man says: 'I'm a close neighbour of yours, for I live inside Hvammsgil Ravine, and I was just coming back from the sea, like you. I'm too poor to pay you as well as I ought for giving me a hand, but this much good I can do you, if you follow my advice – you need never again make a useless journey down to the sea, on the one condition that you never go down before you see me go. Then it can't fail; you'll always be able to row out every time you go down, if only you keep this condition.'

The farmer thanks him for this advice. And so, while three years went by, he never set out until after he had seen his neighbour go past, and never made a useless journey, and never failed to make a catch. But when three years had passed, it happened one day that very early in the morning the weather was perfect for fishing, and everyone went straight down to the sea, but the farmer did not see his neighbour go down, though he waited a long while. Finally he could stand it no longer, and went, without his neighbour having come. But when the farmer did reach the sea, all the boats had rowed away. That day, all the boats were lost in a storm, but this farmer was not harmed, as he had been too late for any boat that morning.

But that night the farmer dreamed of his neighbour, who spoke these words to him; 'You can thank me for one good thing at least, that you did not put out to sea today! But because you set out without having seen me, you need never wait here for me again, as I don't mean to let you see me again, now that you didn't follow my advice.'

And indeed the farmer never set eyes on his neighbour again.

J.Á. I 6–7 (*Sjóma>urinn á Götum*); from Runófur Jónsson, from a story current in Mýrdalur. As fairies are often thought to make their living by the same type of work as their human neighbours, those of fishing districts (e.g. in the Isle of Man or the Faroes) are naturally fishers too. Communication with elves through dreams is common in Icelandic tales and beliefs.

THE ELFIN WOMAN IN CHILDBIRTH

Away in the East Quarter – in Oddi, so it is said – a young servant girl went out to the churchyard one evening to fetch in the washing, and while she was busy collecting it, up came a man whom she did not know. He takes her by the hand and tells her to come with him, and says he will do her no harm – 'But if you won't do it', says he, 'you'll find your luck has changed for the worse.'

The girl dared not disobey his orders, so she goes along with him until they come to a farmhouse (or so it seemed to her, but in fact it was a knoll). Then they go to the door of this farm and he leads her in, and along a long passage, until they come to the main room. The far end of the room looked dim before her eyes, but at the nearer end there was a light burning, and there she saw a woman lying on the floor, and she was screaming, and could not give birth to her child. She saw an old woman by her, who was very distressed.

The man who had brought her there said: 'Go to my wife and help her, so that she can give birth to her child.'

The girl went to where the woman lay, and the old woman went away; then the girl ran her hands over the woman on the floor in the way which she knew was needed, and she very quickly was released from her trouble, so that the child was born at once.

As soon as the child was born, the father came with a glass bottle, and told her to put some stuff from it in the child's eyes, but to take care not to let it get into her own eyes. She did indeed put some stuff from the bottle into the child's eyes, but when she had done so she rubbed her finger over one of her own eyes. Then with this eye she saw that there were many people at the far end of the room. The man took the glass bottle back and went off with it; then he returned, and thanked her for her help, and so did the woman, and they told her she would become a very lucky woman. He puts a roll of cloth in her apron, so fine that she had never seen the like;

then he takes her by the hand and leads her till they come to the churchyard from which he had fetched her, and then he goes away, and she sets off home.

The very next winter the wife of the priest there died, and this girl afterwards became his wife. She often said she could see the Hidden People; also, whenever she saw them building their hay-cocks she would have her own hay built into cocks too, and sure enough it would shortly start raining, even though the sky had been clear before.

One day she went to market with her husband the priest. While she was in a trader's booth she saw the elf-man she had once met, buying goods from a merchant of the Hidden People who was there too. Then she made a blunder, for she went up to him and said: 'Good luck go with you, friend! I thank you for your kindness last time'. But at this he walked up to her, put his finger in his mouth and drew it across her eyes, and at once her power of sight changed, so that from then on she never again saw the Hidden People, nor any of their doings.

J.Á. I 15–16, from the writings (c.1830) of Ólafur Sveinsson of Purkey (1780–1845); he collected elf legends in the early nineteenth century, in order to prove the existence of elves, in which he himself fully believed. This tale is a good example of ML 5070, 'Midwife to the Fairies', well known in Scandinavia, the British Isles, and elsewhere (Simpson 1988, 212–13; Kvideland and Sehmsdorf, 227–8).

Jón Árnason gives four other versions (116–20; for one of them, see the next story, and for another, see Craigie 143–5). He also has two stories about persons who refused to help, or who helped inefficiently, and were punished for it (J.Á. I 21–3). The motif first appears in Iceland in the four-teenth-century *Gǫngu-Hrólfs saga*, and becomes common from the end of the sixteenth century.

The woman's greeting to the elf on seeing him in the market is here motivated by good manners; 'thank you for last time' is an essential phrase on re-encountering one's former host or hostess.

Dr Skapti Sæmundsson

There was a man called Skapti Sæmundsson; his mother was called Gudrid, and at the time when this story took place they were living at Bondholl in Myrar, and Skapti was only a young boy. When the weather was fine in summer, he used to act as shepherd, or do jobs of that sort. One spring, when he was somewhere between seven and nine years old, he used to be sent to see to the lambs in the pens; it is the usual custom in that district to go out to the sheep-folds early in the morning to milk the ewes and let the lambs out of the pens. Skapti was a very early riser and would get up first thing in the morning to do this, and then when he came back his parents would let him lie on his bed again while his mother got on with preparing a meal.

One morning, as so often, when he had come in from the sheep-folds and his mother was busy, he lay down on his bed fully dressed, but took his shoes off; it was past six, but before nine. Shortly afterwards, his mother saw him go past the dairy door and along the path; she thought he couldn't get to sleep and had gone out for some reason, so she paid no particular attention. After a curiously long time had gone by, she sees him coming back to the main building, and thinks he has been out longer than usual. But she thought no more about it till later, when she goes into the main room, and Skapti is sleeping now, and his shoes are lying at the foot of the bed just as she would expect, but he had put his right hand outside the bedclothes, and there is a great smear of dry blood running obliquely across the knuckles. But she does not worry over it, for she sees that the blood is dry.

As soon as he wakes, she asks how there comes to be blood on his hand, and whether he had hurt himself. He said no, and that he knew nothing about it, but then he noticed that there was dry blood all over the palm of his hand too. So, as Skapti was a wise lad even at an early age, he said, when he had sat silent for a while:

'Perhaps there is some connection between this blood and my dream earlier today.'

Then he tells how he thought that an elderly woman wearing a kerchief came to him in his sleep and asked him to go with her. He said he did so, and when he and she had gone a little way beyond the homefield at Bondholl, there in front of them was a small farmhouse which he did not know; the woman asked him to step inside, for she wanted to ask him to help her daughter, who was lying in labour.

Skapti went indoors with her, and into the main room; at one end there were three beds, but at the other only one, and in this one lay a girl, and she was screaming. As soon as he comes in there, the lad says he knows nothing about such matters, being just a child. The older woman says there was not much he need do. Then she takes hold of Skapti's right hand and lays it on the girl's lower belly, and she is released from her trouble so rapidly that she gives birth to her child at once.

Then the older woman sees Skapti out and thanks him warmly for his help, but says she is too poor to reward him as much as would be right – 'But this I do say,' says she, 'that you will always have good luck as a healer.' After which, she and her farm vanished.

People then realised how the blood got on the boy's hand, and that this must have been an elf-woman. Her words were thought to have come true, for Skapti was always considered a lucky healer when he grew up, and when he was called to a woman in childbirth he never failed to find a way to help her. When Skapti was twenty-four he moved to Reykjavík, and stayed there till the day of his death.

J.Á. I 19–20. Skapti Sæmundsson lived from 1768 to 1821, and it was his own son Skapti Skaptason who was Jón Árnason's informant, he having heard the story from his grandmother when he was a child. A similar instance of this legend being used to bolster the prestige of a doctor is recorded in R. Grant Stewart, *Popular Superstitions of the Highlands*, 1823; a doctor then practising in Strathspey used to claim that skill in midwifery was a gift bestowed on his family ever since his great-grandmother helped a fairy woman in childbirth.

Playing 'Blind Beggar'

It happened on a certain farm that some children had gone out to play beside a knoll; there was one little girl, and two boys older than her. They saw a hole in the knoll, and then this girl who was the youngest among them took it into her head to stick her hand right inside the hole, and to say as a joke, as children often do:

> *The old man's blind, the old man's blind,*
> *Lay a little something in the old man's hand!*

Then a large gilded button for her apron was laid in the child's hand.

As soon as the other children saw this, they were jealous. Then the eldest stuck his hand right in and said the same as the youngest had said, and he expected that this would get him some trinket at least as fine as she had got. But it did not work out like that, for this boy received nothing at all; and, what's more, when he took his hand out of the hole it had withered, and so it remained all his life.

J.Á. I 28–9 (*'Legg í lófa karls, karls'*), from Ólafur Sveinsson of Purkey. The game mentioned here is much the same as English children's 'Open your mouth and shut your eyes, And you will have a nice surprise', offering similar opportunities for niceness – or nastiness. This story is a variant of AT 503: 'The Gifts of the Little People'. Supernatural beings are always quick to punish greed and jealousy; moreover, Icelandic elves resent ill-mannered intrusions on their privacy (J.Á. I 4). The first child acted in innocence, not realising that the knoll was an elf's home; the others knew perfectly well what it was, and their motives were in any case unworthy. The same point is made in a recently collected English variant from Somerset (Briggs 1970, I 279–80).

LAPPA, THE ELFIN COW

On a farm in the west, the cowman went out one winter day soon after waking, as he usually did, to see to the cows before the milkmaid went to them. When he went in, there were four cows standing in the middle of the floor; he assumed that these were the cows that ought to be in the stalls, and that they had all broken loose. The man was hot-tempered by nature, and would never stop to think when he grew angry. So now he grips one cow roughly by the ear, meaning to get her into a stall, but she was unwilling, and in his sudden rage he bites her so hard on the backbone that blood gushed out. But at this moment the girl who was to do the milking came into the cow-house with a light and asked what was going on, for she could hear the cowman cursing, and a great commotion in the cow-house.

As soon as the light came into the cow-house, the man saw that the cows were in their stalls where they ought to be, and there were no more of them inside the building than there ought to be, except for the one he was struggling with, and which he had bitten in his rage; she made one too many. But the other three were gone.

The girl asked what it all meant. He said he did not know, and told her what he had found when he first came into the cow-house, how he had thought it was his own cows standing in the middle, and that they had all broken loose; how he had lost his temper with them and seized the one he was still holding now, meaning to get her into a stall, but had not managed to do so; but into the stalls themselves, said he, he had not gone.

'You were wrong to act as you did,' said the girl, 'and I'm afraid no good will come to you from this.'

Then she goes indoors and tells the farmer, and he thought what had happened was most unlucky, and so now he goes out to the cow-house and scolds the cowman. He also wanted to turn the cow out, but she would not go away, so after a while she was put into an empty stall. This cow had her udder full, and a big one it was; he told the girl to milk her, but she could not get much out of her. Then the farmer's wife tried, and the same thing happened, and the cow turned savage; for two days this went on, and they could not get much out of her.

Towards evening of the second day that the cow had been there, the farmer's wife was still in the cow-house after the rest had gone in, and she had no light with her. When she had been there a while, she heard someone come in at the door and pass through the cow-house to the stall where this cow was, and then come back and out again, but she herself went back to the house. Later, at milking time, the housewife went to the cow-house herself, and when she went to milk this newly-arrived cow, the cow behaved just as she had done before.

Then the woman heard a voice at the cow-house window:

> There, there, Lappa dear,
> Your poor dugs are sore, I fear;
> That's because the women here
> Never stroke you, Lappa dear.

Then the woman began to stroke the cow and call her by her own name as she heard her named in the rhyme spoken by the elf-woman at the window. She could milk her then, for she stood quiet, and she got a lot of milk from her. It is not said that any harm came to her or her husband, but the cowman had little luck. Many cows are descended from this one, and it was commonly said of them that they were 'of Lappa's breed'.

J.Á. I 138–9 ('Ló, ló, mín Lappa'), from Ólafur Sveinsson of Purkey. A variant of this tale and its verse was included in a Latin work by the Revd Þorsteinn Björnsson (d. 1675); it has many parallels in Norway (ML 6055, 'The Fairy Cows'). The idea that an elfin cow can be captured by drawing blood recurs in a closely similar tale (J.Á. I 37, tr. Craigie 156–7); mermen too have fine cows, and these are to be captured by breaking a bladder on their muzzles (see pp. 108–9). Fairy cattle, often associated with water, are well known in British and Irish traditions (Briggs 1967, 77–8).

THE CHANGELING WHO STRETCHED

At one time two households shared the farm of Sogn in Kjos, and one of these two men had a son who was thought to be not quite right in the head. He never learnt to speak or to use his hands properly or do anything active, but lay in bed all day, though as regards food he was as greedy as could be. People rather suspected that the lad was a changeling, but for a long time it was not certain.

When this lad had reached the usual age of Confirmation, it so happened one winter day that everyone had left the house to see to the cattle, except for this boy, who was lying on his bed as usual, and the mother of the other family, who was lying ill in bed with a child at her side, and this was all in the one room. After the others had gone out, the sick woman heard how the boy was seized with such a fit of yawning that she began to feel rather worried, and the noises he was making gave her the shivers. Next, she hears him begin to jerk about on his bed and stretch himself; then all at once she realises that he is standing up in bed and stretching and stretching himself, till he is touching the roof-beams. It was a room with raised floor-boards, and with short cross-ties high up between the rafters.

Then his fit of yawning comes on him once more, and for a while he stands leaning his face against one of the cross-ties, and this tie-beam was right inside his open mouth as he gaped and yawned, for he opened his jaws so wide that the upper jaw rested on top of the

39

beam and the lower appeared below it. At the same time he grew so abominably ugly and loathsome to look at that the woman was scared to death and screamed with terror at seeing him, and at realising that she was alone in the room with him – and indeed she remained easily frightened for a long while after this unlucky sight.

But as soon as the woman screamed, he collapsed as if he'd been shot, and flung himself back down into his bed and turned back to what he had been before, before the people came back indoors from the cattle-sheds. However, after this everyone thought there was no doubt at all that this boy was a changeling.

J.Á. I 41–2 (*Umskiptíngurinn í Sogni*), from Ragnhei> and Ragnhild Einarsdœtr (b.1829). This tale shows well how the concept of 'changeling' could become attached to a mental defective, and the way in which a sick and easily frightened woman's nightmare or feverish illusion could be taken for reality. The form her 'experience' takes can be paralleled in legends of some other Scandinavian and Slavonic areas, for instance in Swedish tales of changelings who, thinking themselves alone, leave their cradles, grow huge, and try to steal food or to rape a girl (Hartmann, 80–1).

'LET US TAKE HIM!'

Two elfin women once went to a farm to leave a changeling there. They came to where the baby they wished to take was; it was lying in a cradle, and there was nobody nearby except for another child, which was two years old.

The younger and less cautious of the elf-women goes straight up to the cradle and says:

Let us take him, take him, do!

Then the elder says:

> *We can't, for that would harm us too:*
> *A cross above, beneath, they drew;*
> *And by him sits a child of two,*
> *And he will speak of what we do.*

At that they went off without doing anything, partly because of the cross marks which had been made over the cradle and also beneath the baby before it was laid there, and partly also because of the two-year-old child who was sitting by the cradle, and who later told everyone what had happened.

J.Á. I 43–4; a tale common throughout Iceland. The protective devices mentioned here, the crosses and the presence of an older child, were commonly believed in and practised; a third device was to lay in the cradle a Bible open at the Gospel of St. John. Once a baby had cut its first tooth, it was usually thought to be safe from being exchanged for a changeling (but see p.43), though elves might still try to lure it away (see pp.45–7). Correspondingly, in certain more detailed and realistic accounts of the physical appearance and behaviour of children reputed to be changelings, one can recognise mental defects and physical disorders which reveal themselves soon after birth (e.g. hydrocephalus). See also Simpson 1988, 192–6; Kvideland and Sehmsdorf, 207–12; for British changeling beliefs and tales, see Briggs 1967, 115–19; Briggs 1978, 104–7.

MAKING A CHANGELING

Kristin Finnsdottir, who lived at Minni-Thvera around 1830–40, used to tell a story about her mother, who had the second sight. The story was that she was once out in the meadows with her own mother, Kristin's grandmother, and saw two women coming down from the fells and leading between them an old man, who was carrying something. When they got nearer they untied this bundle from the old man's back, and then she saw that it was a cradle with a red cot-cover over it. After this, they seized the old man and beat him, so that he began to get smaller and smaller, and turned into a little boy. Then they took him again and kneaded him, till he had become as small as a little baby. Then they laid him in the cradle, carried it between them, and so headed straight for the farm, with cradle and changeling and all.

The girl told her mother what she had seen, and the mother at once turned and ran home, and reached her baby's cradle (which she had left standing outside in front of the house) before the women of the Hidden People got to it. But as soon as the Hidden Women saw this, they took the child they had with them out of its cradle, and smacked it and slapped it and drove it away from them. At that, their old man began to grow and grow again at a furious pace, until he was just as he had been originally; and off he went with them into the fells, and there they all disappeared.

J.Á. I 44–5 (*Barnsvaggan á Minni-*fi*verá*), from an account written in 1848 by the Revd Jón Jónsson Nor>mann on information given by Kristín Fornadóttir. As elves were thought of as the same size as human adults, it is only logical that the wizened, toothless old elves who were to be left as changelings should be reduced in size by some means; this too is why changelings were thought to need to stretch from time to time. The point about the red coverlet is that red is a typical fairy colour in Iceland; so is blue. This story, like the next, stresses the danger of leaving a small child unattended even for a few moments; fairy beliefs could often serve to reinforce good principles of mothercraft and housekeeping (cf. Thomas, 612).

FATHER OF EIGHTEEN ELVES

On a farm one summer it happened that everybody was out in the fields except the mistress herself, who stayed at home to mind the house, with her son, who was three or four years old. This boy had grown and thriven well up to this time; he was talking already, was intelligent, and seemed a most promising child. Now, as the woman had various chores to do besides minding her child, she had to turn her back on him for a little while and go down to a stream near the house to wash some churns. She left him in the doorway, and there is nothing to tell until she came back after a brief while. As soon as she spoke to him, he shrieked and howled in a more vicious and ugly way than she ever expected, for up till then he had been a very placid child, affectionate and likeable, but now all she got was squalling and shrieks. This went on for some time; the child never spoke one word, but was so terribly wilful and moody that the woman did not know what to do about the change in him; moreover, he stopped growing, and began to look quite like an imbecile.

The mother was very upset over it all, and she decides to go and see a neighbour of hers who was thought to be a wise woman and to know a great deal, and she tells her her troubles. The neighbour questions her closely, asking how long it is since the child began to be so unmanageable, and how she thought the change had begun. The mother tells her just what had happened.

When this wise neighbour had heard the whole story, she says: 'Don't you think, my dear, that the child is a changeling? It's my opinion that he was exchanged while you left him alone in the doorway.'

'I don't know,' says the mother. 'Can't you teach me some way to get at the truth?'

'So I can,' says the other. 'You must leave the child by himself some time, and arrange for something really extraordinary to happen in front of him, and then he will say something when he sees there is no one near by. But you must listen secretly to know what he says, and if the boy's words seem at all odd or suspicious, whip him unmercifully until something happens.'

With this, they broke off their talk, and the mother thanked her neighbour for her good advice, and went home.

As soon as she gets back, she sets down a tiny pot in the middle of the kitchen floor; then she takes several broom handles and ties them end to end until the top end is poking right up the kitchen chimney, and to the bottom end she ties the porridge stirring-stick, and this she sets upright in the little pot. As soon as she had rigged up this contraption in the kitchen, she fetched the child in and left him alone there; then she left the room, but stood listening outside, where she could peep in through the crack of the door.

She had not been long gone when she sees the child start waddling round and round the pot with the porridge-stick in it and studying it carefully; and in the end the child says: 'I'm old enough now, as my whiskers show, and I'm a father with eighteen children of my own in Elfland, and yet never in my life have I seen so long a pole in so small a pot!'

At that, the woman runs back in with a good birch, seizes the changeling, and beats him long and unmercifully, and then he howls most horribly.

When she had been whipping him for some while, she sees a woman who was a stranger to her coming into the kitchen with a little boy in her arms, and a sweet pretty child he is.

This stranger gives the child a loving look, and says to the mother: 'We don't act fairly by one another; I cuddle your child, but you beat my husband.'

Saying this, she puts down this child, the housewife's own son, and leaves him there; but she takes her old man off with her, and the two of them disappear. But the boy grew up with his own mother, and turned out a fine man.

J.Á. I 42–3; a story common throughout Iceland. This is the widespread European tale (ML 5085, 'The Changeling') of a changeling startled into revealing his age by some grotesque device (e.g. boiling water in eggshells or making a monstrous sausage), and subsequently driven off by harsh treatment. The huge porridge-stirrer is a popular motif in Norwegian variants, while the elf-woman's reproach is a standard feature in Denmark – 'I have not been as brutal to your child as you to mine', she says to the human mother, as the latter roasts the changeling on a hot stove. The changeling's age here is minimal when compared with the long time-span calculated by the growth and decay of forests in some versions, or by reincarnations in others; one Danish changeling says, 'I am so old that I have been suckled by eighteen mothers'. For general discussions, see Hartland 93–134, Hartmann 76–86, Briggs 1967, 115–19. See also Simpson (1988), 195; Kvideland and Sehmsdorf, 209–10; Thorpe, 460–1; a close English parallel is in E.M. Leather, *The Folk-Lore of Herefordshire* (London, 1912), 46–7.

THE CHILD AND THE ELF-WOMAN

At Heidarbot in the district of Thingey, it happened one evening that while a woman was out in the cow-house one of her children left the house, meaning to follow her there. As soon as the child goes outside, he sees her standing in the flagged court-yard; she beckons him in silence, tapping her thigh to call him, and gently, very gently, she walks away, tapping her thigh and beckon-ing him to follow. There are some sharp crags above that farm, which are called Stoplar, 'The Steeples'. Towards these crags the woman goes, and lures the child to go with her; then she disappears into the Steeples with him, for she was not the child's true mother, but an elf.

Now the next thing to say is that the woman comes out of the cow-house, finds her child is missing, and asks where it is – but the people indoors said he was out in the cow-house with his mother. The parents were horrified; men gathered and went searching, but he was not to be found, wherever they searched.

At Sand there lived a man named Arnor, who was believed to be a magician. The mother went to him to ask advice, and arrived late in the day. Arnor asked her to stay the night, and she agreed; he asked her at what time the child had disappeared, and she told him. So that evening, at about the same hour, Arnor takes a knife and cuts three triangular bits of board, from the flooring of the main room. But as he was cutting the last one, a loud crash was heard. Then he put the pieces back in their places, and told the woman she need not be afraid to sleep soundly that night, for her child had come back.

Next day she went home, and her child had indeed come back. Something which everyone thought strange was that one of his cheeks was black and blue, and that afterwards this bruise never faded away.

So now the child was asked where he had been, and he told them about the woman he thought was his mother, and how he had followed her, crying and calling 'Mummy!', until she came to the foot of the Steeples, when she caught him in her arms and carried him inside the Steeples, where she tried to treat him kindly, but he could see now that it was not his mother. He ate no food in her home, for to him it all looked red. But on the evening when Arnor cut the floorboards, three stones came crashing down from the mountain, all three triangular. At the third one, the elf-woman picked the child up; she was very angry, and she ran all the way back to the farm with him, and at parting she gave him a good slap on the cheek – and that was the loud crash that had been heard after the third piece of board was cut out. Because of this, one cheek of his was black and blue.

The child's name was Gudmund, and later he lived in the North Quarter; he had a daughter called Elizabeth, who married and raised a family in Eyjafjord.

J.Á. I 48–9; a story current in Eyjafjör>ur. There are many Icelandic tales, of varying degrees of elaboration, about children and young people taken away by elves and subsequently recovered (J.Á. I 45–55), and such beliefs go back at least to the sixteenth century (Sveinsson 1940, 77–9; 2003, 84–6). Children lost and found again in this way are often said to have been found in some highly inaccessible spot among the mountains. The taboo on Otherworld food is a recurrent motif; so is the blow leaving an indelible mark. Abducted adults sometimes return on their own, but sometimes need to be rescued by someone with supernatural powers. In one such tale a girl is summoned home by a bishop and then held firmly in a strong man's grip despite her pleas and ravings (J.Á. I 57–9, tr. Powell and Magnússon 46–9); in another, a man begs a priest to call his daughter back, but changes his mind when he sees in a vision that her face is now blue, which is a sign that she has ceased to be a human being (J.Á. I 56–7, tr. Craigie 150–1). The girls carried off in this way may later send for a human midwife, or for a priest to baptise their half-elfin baby, or may be brought home for burial after dying in childbirth (J.Á. I 54, 73–7).

Similar abduction tales are common in Norwegian and Swedish lore; the process is called *bergtagning*, 'taking into the mountains', and the victims are children, women soon after childbirth, and marriageable young men and women whose work takes them near the mountains, such as woodcutters, charcoal burners, and dairymaids on the upland pastures (Simpson 1988, 207–11; Kvideland and Sehmsdorf, 212–20). Those who return often show physical or mental damage (Hartmann, 98 ff.). The belief that children might be carried off for a few days by benevolent fairies was still strong in the Faroes in the 1940s (Williamson, 249).

The seer mentioned in the present tale is a real person, Arnór or Arnflór Ólafsson, who lived in the seventeenth century. Several other anecdotes tell how he tried to recover children from the elves, how he acted as midwife to an elf-woman, how another elf-woman advised and protected him, and how the elves at last got his body (J.Á. I 603–5); in one of these tales he is said to have caused a rock-fall to punish elves who had abducted a child. He is also said to have outwitted a ghost and pinned it under a stake (J.Á. I 299).

THE CHURCH BUILDER AT REYNIR

There once lived a certain farmer at Reynir in Myrdal. It was his task to build a church there, but he had met with delays in getting timber, and now haymaking time had come but no carpenters had been found, so he began to fear that the church would not be up before winter.

One day he was strolling gloomily through his meadow, when a man came up and offered to build the church for him; the farmer was to tell him what his name was before the work was finished, or else the farmer was to hand over his only son, who was six. They struck the bargain on these terms.

The stranger set to work; he never concerned himself with anything but the building, and was a man of very few words, and indeed the work went ahead so remarkably fast that the farmer saw it would be finished at the same time as the haymaking. Then the farmer grew wretched, but there was nothing he could do.

In autumn, when the church was almost complete, the farmer wandered out beyond his meadow, and threw himself down on some knoll out there. Then, from inside the knoll, he heard a verse that a mother was singing to her child and this was it:

> *He's coming home from Reynir,*
> *Finn, your own daddy;*
> *He's bringing you a playmate,*
> *A fine little laddy.*

This verse was repeated over and over again.

The farmer now felt far more cheerful, and went back to the church. There the builder was busy shaping the last plank above the altar, and was about to nail it in place.

The farmer said: 'You'll soon have finished, my friend Finn!'

The builder was so taken aback by this remark that he flung the plank down and disappeared, and he has never been seen again since.

J.Á. I 58, from the Revd Skúli Gíslason (d.1888), from a tale current in southern and eastern Iceland. This is ML 7065, 'Building a Church: the Name of the Master Builder'. It is less common in Iceland than in Norway and Sweden, where the villain is usually an ogre who demands the sun and moon and/or the hero's eyes or life. In Norway the hero is often St Olav and the building is Trondheim Cathedral; the first printed reference to the story is from 1704 (Craigie 390–2, Christiansen 1964, 5–7, Simpson 1988, 28–9). In Sweden the hero is St Laurentius, and the building is Lund Cathedral (Lindow, 86–8). The story does not always have a religious dimension; in Scotland it is told about the building of Stirling Castle and Edinburgh Castle (MacDonald, 63).

The earliest instance of the central motif in Scandinavia is the myth in Snorri Sturluson's *Edda* (*c.*1220) about a giant who offered to build Asgard in return for the sun and moon and the goddess Freyja, but was foiled when Loki lured away his horse, which dragged the stones for him. A challenge to name-guessing (Motif H 521) is also the leading feature of the international wonder-tale AT 500, 'Tom Tit Tot' or 'Rumpelstiltskin'.

THE GIRL AT THE SHIELING

There was once a priest in the North Quarter who had brought up a little girl as his own. The summer pastures belonging to his farm were high up in the fells, and he always sent his sheep and cattle there in the summer with the herdsmen, and with a woman to keep house for them. When his foster-daughter grew up, she became the housekeeper at this shieling, and was as good at this as at everything — for she was a skilful girl, and beautiful, and had many accomplishments. Many well-to-do men asked for her hand, for she was thought the best match in the North Quarter, but she refused all offers. One day the priest spoke seriously to his adopted daughter and urged her to marry, saying he would not always be there to look after her, for he was an old man. She took it very badly, and said she had no fancy for such things, and was very happy as she was, and that there was no luck in marriage. So they said no more about it, for the time being.

As that winter wore on, people thought the girl was getting rather plump below the belt, and the plumpness grew more and more marked as time went on. In spring her foster-father spoke to her again, and urged her to tell him how things were with her, and said she must surely be with child, and should not go up to the shieling that summer. She strongly denied that she was pregnant, and said there was nothing the matter with her, and that she would see to her housekeeping that summer just as before. When the pastor saw he was getting nowhere, he let her have her way, but he told the men who were to be in the shieling never to go out at any time leaving her quite alone, and this they promised faithfully. So then they all moved up to the shieling, and the girl was as merry as could be.

So time passed, and nothing noteworthy happened. The men at the shieling kept strict watch on their housekeeper and never left her alone. One evening it happened that a shepherd found that all the sheep and cows were missing, and so every living soul left the shieling except the housekeeper, who stayed behind alone. The search-party searched very late and did not find the beasts till almost morning, for it was very misty. When they came home, the housekeeper was up and about, and she was brisker in her movements and lighter on her feet than she had usually been. The men also saw, as time went by, that her plumpness had lessened, though they could not tell how, and so they thought that it must have been some other kind of swelling, and not pregnancy.

So home they went from the shieling in autumn, the whole company of men and beasts. The priest saw then that the housekeeper was far slimmer in the waist than she had been the previous winter, so then he went to the men who had been at the shieling and asked whether they had disobeyed his orders and left the girl quite alone. They told him the truth, that they had once all left her to go out searching for their beasts, as these had all gone missing. The pastor grew angry, and wished bad luck on all who had disregarded his orders, for he said he had suspected as much as soon as the girl went off to the shieling in spring.

Next winter a man came to ask the hand of the priest's foster-daughter, and she was not at all pleased about it, but the priest told her she would not avoid marrying him, for he was a fine man and everyone spoke well of him. He had inherited his father's farm that spring, and his mother ran the house for him. So this marriage was settled, whether the girl liked or not, and their wedding was held next spring at the priest's house.

But before the woman put her bridal dress on, she said to her betrothed: 'Before you go ahead and marry me against my wishes, I lay down one condition – that you never take strangers in to lodge for the winter, without first telling me, or else things will go wrong for you.' And this the man promised.

So the wedding feast was held, and she went home with her husband and took over the running of his home, but her heart was not in it, for she was never cheerful or happy-looking, though her husband pampered her and would not have her working her fingers to the bone.

Every summer she used to stay at home when the others were out haymaking, and her mother-in-law would stay to keep her company and to see to the housekeeping with her. Between whiles they would sit knitting or spinning, and the older woman would tell her stories to amuse her. One day when the old woman had ended a story, she told her daughter-in-law that she ought to tell a story now. But she said that she did not know any. The other pressed her hard, and so she promised to tell her the only one she knew, and so she began her tale:

'There was once a girl on a farm who was housekeeper at the shieling. Not far from the shieling there were great rocky scarps, and she often went walking near them. There was a man of the Hidden Folk who lived inside these scarps, and they soon got acquainted and grew to love one another dearly. He was so good and kind to the girl that he would refuse her nothing, and would follow her wishes in everything. But the upshot was that when some time had gone by the girl became pregnant; the head of her household accused her of it when she was about to go to the shieling the following summer, but the girl denied it, and went to the shieling as usual. But he ordered the others who were to be at the shieling never to go off and leave her alone, and they promised. They did all leave her, however, to search for their cattle, and then the pangs of childbirth came on her. The man who had been her lover came then, and sat beside her, and he cut the cord and washed the baby and swaddled it. Then, before he went off with the child, he gave her a drink from a flask, and it was the sweetest drink which I ever —' at that moment the ball of knitting wool slipped from her hand, so she bent down for it, and corrected herself '— which *she* had ever tasted, that's what I meant to say, and so she was well again in a moment, after all her pains. From that hour they never saw one another again, she and the man of the Hidden Folk; but she was married off to another man, much against her will, for she pined bitterly for her first lover, and from that time she never knew one happy day. And so ends this story.'

The mother-in-law thanked her for the story, and took good care to remember it. And so things went on for some time, and nothing notable happened, and the woman went on being sad, in her usual way, but was good to her husband all the same.

One summer when the mowing was almost done, two men came up to the farmer; one was tall, the other short, and both wore broad-brimmed hats so that one could hardly see their faces. The taller one spoke up, asking the farmer to take them in for the winter. He said he never took anyone in without his wife knowing, and that he would go and speak to her before promising them lodgings. The tall one said this was a ridiculous thing to say, that such a fine, masterful man was so henpecked that he couldn't make up his mind on a little matter like giving two men bed and board for one winter. So they settled the matter, and the farmer promised these men their winter quarters without asking his wife's leave.

That evening the strangers arrive at the farmer's house, and he assigns them their quarters in a building on the outskirts of the farm, and tells them to stay there. Then he goes to his wife, and tells her how matters stand. She took it very badly, saying that this had been the first favour she had ever asked him, and it would probably be the last, and that as he had taken them in on his own, he could see to everything they might need all winter on his own; and so the conversation ended.

Now all was quiet until one day that autumn, when the farmer and his wife were meaning to go to Holy Communion. It was the custom in those days, as it long was in some parts of Iceland, that those who mean to go to Communion should go to all the people in the house, kiss them and beg their forgiveness if they had offended them. Up till then, the mistress of the house had always avoided the lodgers and not let them see her, and so on this occasion likewise she did not go to greet them.

She and her husband set out, but as soon as they were beyond the fence, he said to her: 'You did of course greet our lodgers, didn't you?'

She said no.

He told her not to commit such a sin as to go off without greeting them.

'You show me in many ways that you care nothing for me,' said she. 'First by the fact that you took these men in without my leave, and now again when you want to force me to kiss them. All the same, I will obey; but you'll be sorry for it, for my life is at stake, and yours too, very likely.'

Now she turns back homewards, and is a very long time gone. Now the farmer too goes back home, and goes to where he expects the lodgers to be, and there he finds them, in their own quarters. He sees the taller lodger and the mistress of the house both lying on the floor dead, in one another's arms, and they had died of grief. The other was standing by them, weeping, when the farmer came in, but he soon disappeared, and nobody knew where he went.

From the story which the wife had told her mother-in-law, people felt sure that the tall stranger must have been the elf she had made love with in the shieling, and the small one who disappeared, her son and his.

J.Á. I 64–7, from Helga Benediktsdóttir (d. 1855). Two variants of this tale are in J.Á. I 67–70 and 70–2, the latter tr. in Powell and Magnússon 58–65. It also appears in *Ólafs saga Þórhallasonar* (*c*.1788), by Eiríkur Laxdal. Pathetic love between a girl and an elf is the subject of the sixteenth-century poem *Kötludraumur* and lullaby *Ljúflingsmál*; the latter is said to have been taught by an elf to a human girl who had borne his child but could not hush its weeping. *Ljúflingur* is a synonym for 'elf', and is related to *ljúfur*, 'beloved', 'darling'. That elves should try to trick girls on lonely mountain pastures into marrying them is a common theme in Norwegian and Swedish tales, but there the attempt is almost always foiled (ML 6005, 'The Interrupted Fairy Wedding'). The tender pathos of the Icelandic tales, with their stress on the girl's enduring love for the elf and her conflicting loyalties, gives them a highly individual tone. The nearest English equivalents are tales like 'Cherry of Zennor', in which a human servant girl loves her fairy master, and pines when he dismisses her (Briggs 1971, I 199–202, 234, 244–7).

THE RED-HEADED WHALE

One day some men from Sudurnes rowed out to the Geirfugla Skerry to trap auks there, but when they were wanting to set off for home once more, one man was missing. They hunted all over the skerry for him, but he was not to be found, so his companions went home leaving matters as they stood.

A year later, the men from Sudurnes went again to the skerry to trap birds, and then they found the man; he was walking to and fro on the skerry, as cheerful as could be. Some elves had lured the man to them by magic and kept him among them for a year, and had treated him well; they had wanted him to stay longer, but he had not wished to. Now the fact of the matter was that an elf-woman was with child by him, and that he had got permission to leave the skerry and go home on the condition that he promised to arrange for the child to be baptised as soon as it was brought to a church. The woman said she would bring it to Hvalsnes Church, for that was the man's parish church. So now he sailed back to the mainland with those men from Sudurnes, and everyone was glad to see him again.

So now time passed, and nothing worth mentioning happened. Then one Sunday when people came to Hvalsnes for the service, there was a cradle standing outside the church door, and a small baby in it. Over the cradle lay a coverlet, very beautiful and delicately worked, and woven of some unknown cloth; and at the foot of the cradle was a slip of paper with these words written on it; 'He who is the father of this child will see to it that it is baptised.'

The people were all astonished at this event, but no one would acknowledge that he was the father or claim the child as his. The priest had his suspicions about the man who had been missing for a whole year, for he thought the present affair was no stranger than the idea that a man could stay alive out on the skerry, and so he thought that this man be the child's father, or, at the least, must know something about it. But the man replied gruffly that he was not the child's father, and did not care in the least what became of it.

While they were still arguing, up came a tall, stately woman. She was extremely angry, and snatching the coverlet from the cradle she flung it in through the church door, saying: 'The church must not lose its dues!' By this act she gave the coverlet to the church, and it has been used ever since as an altar-cloth for Hvalsnes Church, where it is regarded as a very precious treasure.

Then she turned to the man and said: 'This do I say and this curse do I lay: you shall turn into the most vicious whale in the sea, and shall destroy many ships!'

After which the woman disappeared, and so did the cradle with the baby in it, and nobody ever found out any more about them, but it was the general opinion that this must have been the elf-woman from Geirfugla Skerry, and that the man's own story showed that it was so.

But soon after the woman vanished, the man she had cursed went mad and went rushing off. He ran down to the sea and jumped over the cliff called Stakksgnypa, which is between Keflavik and Leira. Then all at once he turned into the most vicious whale, and was known as Red-Head from then on. He was very evil and destructive. He drowned nineteen boatloads of men between Akranes and Seltjarnarnes, where he was always lurking out in the open sea. Among others, Red-Head drowned the son of the priest of Saurbœ on Hvalfjardarstrand and the second son of the priest of Saurbœ on Kjalarnes. These two priests joined forces, for they took the loss of their sons very much to heart, and their chants drew Red-Head all the way up the fjord which separates the two Saurbœs, which ever since then has been called Hvalfjord, 'Whale Fjord', and drew him right up into the lake up on Botnsheidi, which ever since then has been called Hvalvatn, 'Whale Lake'. Then there came a great earth-quake all round that district, because of which the moors round Hvalvatn are called the Quaking Moors. People have thought there was proof that all this really did happen in the fact that at one time one could see a whale's bones beside this lake, and pretty big ones too. But nobody was ever injured by Red-Head after this.

J.Á. I 83–4 (*Rau>höf>i*); a story current round Sudurness. For two close variants, see J.Á. I 84–9; one is tr. in Powell and Magnússon 65–72. These and two other related tales (J.Á. I 89–93; one translated in Simpson 1988, 211–12) centre upon an elf-woman's wish that her half-human child be baptised, and her anger against its father; in each case, a fine cope or altar-cloth in the local church is cited as evidence for the tale. Stories of this type were known to Arngrímur Jónsson the Learned (d.1648), though he refused to credit them. A single parallel is known from Norway, and a few from Scotland (Christiansen 1959, 20–1). Tales in which an abducted human girl sends for a priest to baptise her half-elfin baby (J.Á. I 54–5) show a similar preoccupation with the relationship of elves to Christianity and their prospects of salvation; the theme is reflected in several international story-patterns (cf. ML 5050, 'The Fairies' Prospect of Salvation', and 5055, 'Fairies and the Christian Faith').

The Geirfugla ('Great Auk') skerries are off the south-west of Iceland; heavy and almost continuous surf surrounds them, so that people seeking seabirds or their eggs could only rarely land there, and might have to leave at short notice; to be marooned there meant certain death.

The curse uttered by the elf-woman, an *álög*, is far commoner in Icelandic tales than in the rest of Scandinavia; it is almost certainly a motif borrowed from Ireland (for it has always been frequent in Celtic tales), and is popular in Icelandic sagas from the fourteenth century on. Monster whales play a great part in Icelandic lore (J.Á. I 628–32); they were said to be consciously malevolent, and huge enough to take a whole ship in their jaws. The powers of certain persons, particularly priests and poets, to kill, summon or expel various noxious creatures, is a very common subject in Icelandic lore (cf. pp. 192–4).

HILD, QUEEN OF THE ELVES

Once, there was a farmer living on a certain homestead up among the mountains, but what his name was, or the name of the farm, the story does not tell. He was unmarried, but he had a housekeeper called Hild, and nobody knew anything about her family. She had complete charge of all household matters there, and everything she tackled turned out well. She was well liked by all the farmhands, and by the farmer himself too, though as it happens they never fell in love; she was a placid woman, rather reserved, but pleasant to deal with all the same.

The farmer's affairs flourished except as regards one point, which was that he found it hard to get shepherds, though he was good at rearing sheep and thought his farm was crippled if it had no shepherd. It was not that the farmer was harsh to his shepherds, nor yet that the housekeeper failed to provide what she should for them; the root of the trouble was that they never lived to be old, but were always found dead in bed on Christmas morning.

In those days it was the custom of the country to have a Midnight Mass on Christmas Eve, and to go to church for this was just as much part of observing the festival as going on Christmas Day itself. But out on the hill farms which were far from a church it was no easy matter to go to this service and be there in good time unless one set out from home before the shepherds on such farms could get in from their work. However, on this farm the shepherds did not have to guard the house, although it was always customary for someone to do so on Christmas Eve and New Year's Eve while the rest were at church, because ever since Hild came to the farm she had always offered to do this herself, and at the same time she would see about everything needed for the festival, food and all; she would stay up so far into the night working at all this, that often the people would have come back from their church service and have gone to bed and to sleep before she went to her bed.

After this had been going on for some years, with the farmer's shepherds all coming to a sudden end on Christmas Eve, it gave rise to so much gossip in the district that the farmer had great difficulty in hiring anyone for the work, and the more men died, the worse it got. However, neither he nor his servants were under any suspicion of having caused the shepherds' deaths, for they had all died without a wound. Finally the farmer said he would no longer burden his conscience by hiring shepherds for certain death, and as for what became of his stock of sheep, he would have to leave that to fate.

One day, after he had come to this decision and had quite made up his mind to take no one else into his household, there came a bold, tough-looking man who offered to take service with him.

The farmer said: 'I don't need your services, so I don't want to take you on.'

The stranger said: 'Have you hired a shepherd for your farm next winter?'

The farmer said he had not, and had no intention of ever doing so again – 'You must have heard what fearful fate all my shepherds have met with up to now.'

'I've heard about that,' said the stranger, 'but their doom won't stop me looking after your sheep, if you'll take me on.'

So, as he insisted, the farmer gave in to him and hired him as shepherd. So then time went by, and the farmer and the shepherd got on well with one another, and the others all liked him too, for he was a pleasant fellow to deal with, though he was harsh and fierce enough if there was need for it.

Nothing worth mentioning happened now till Christmas, when, as usual, the farmer and all his people went to church on Christmas Eve, except for the housekeeper, who stayed indoors alone, and the shepherd, who was out with the sheep; the farmer went off leaving her and him behind, each busy in his own way. So the evening wore on till the shepherd came home as usual; he ate his evening meal, and then went to his bed and lay down. It struck him that it would be wiser to stay awake than to sleep, in case something should happen, though he was not in the least afraid, and so he lay awake. When the night was far gone, he heard the others come home from church, take a bite to eat, and go to sleep. He was still none the wiser; but when they were all asleep, as he supposed, he felt his own strength beginning to drain away, as one might well expect in a man tired by his day's work. He thought he would find himself in trouble if sleep overcame him now, so he fought with all his strength to keep alert.

A little time passed, and then he heard someone come up to his bed, and he thought he could make out that it was Hild the housekeeper who was up and about. He pretended to be fast asleep, and felt that she was busy fixing something in his mouth; he realised that it was a magic bridle, but he let her put it on him. As soon as she had bridled him she led him out by the easiest way, got on his back, and rode as hard as she could till she reached a place which looked to him like some sort of deep pit or cleft in the earth. There she dismounted beside a rock and slackened the reins, and having done so disappeared from his view into the cleft. He thought it would be a great pity, and very stupid too, to lose sight of Hild without finding out what became of her. However, he found he could not get far with the bridle on, there was such witchcraft in it, so he hit on the trick of rubbing his head against the rock till he got the bridle off, and leaving it there, and then he leapt down the cleft in which Hild had disappeared.

Before he had gone far down the cleft, he found he could see Hild going ahead; she had reached a beautiful smooth plain, and was crossing it at a rapid pace. All this made him feel sure that there was more to Hild than met the eye, and that there were more tricks up her sleeve than one might suppose in the human world up above. Also, he realised that she would see him at once if he followed her across the plain, so then he took a stone of invisibility which he used to carry about with him, and held it in his left palm; then he put his best foot forward, and ran after her as fast as he could.

When he had gone a long way across this plain, he saw a large and gorgeous hall, and Hild was heading straight up the path towards it. He also saw a crowd of people come out to meet her. Among them was one man who went ahead of the others; he was by far the most richly dressed, and it seemed to the shepherd that as Hild came up this man greeted her as his wife and bade her welcome, while those who were with him hailed her as their queen. With this lordly man there were two children, already well grown, and they welcomed her with great rejoicing as their mother.

When the whole company had greeted the queen, they led her and the king into the hall, where she was welcomed with great honour, dressed in royal robes, and her hands loaded with gold rings. The shepherd followed the crowd into the hall, always keeping as much out of everyone's way as he could, but managing to see all that went on. In this hall he saw the most splendid and costly adornments he had ever set eyes on; there were tables laid and food served, and he was quite amazed at the whole display. After a little, he saw Hild coming into the hall, and she was dressed in the robes described already. The people went to their appointed seats, and Hild took her place on the highseat beside the king, while the rest of the court sat on either hand, and so men feasted for some while. Then the tables were cleared away and the lords and ladies began to dance, those who wished, while others chose whatever pleasures they preferred; but the king and queen talked together, and the shepherd thought their talk seemed full of both love and grief.

While they were talking, three children came up to them, younger than the two who were mentioned earlier, and these too greeted their mother. Queen Hild answered, and lovingly too; she picked the youngest up and sat him on her knee and looked tenderly at him, but he was restless and pestered her with questions. So then the queen set him down again, pulled a ring from her finger, and gave it to him to play with; the child kept quiet then and played with the ring for a while, but lost it on the floor in the end. The shepherd was standing near by; he made a quick move, seized the ring as it fell to the floor, slipped it on and kept it carefully; nobody noticed him, but when the ring was searched for, they all thought it odd that it could not be found.

When the night was far gone, Queen Hild went to get ready to leave; they all begged her to stay longer, and were very sad when they saw her with her travelling clothes on. The shepherd had noticed that in one corner of the hall there sat an old woman, rather evil-looking; of all those present, she was the only one who neither greeted Queen Hild when she arrived nor bade her farewell.

When the king saw Hild in her travelling clothes, and saw she would not stay for all his pleading and the pleading of the rest, he went up to this old woman and said: 'Take back your curse, mother! Listen to my plea, so that my queen need no longer live so far off, nor I have such few short moments of joy with her as we have now.'

The old woman answered angrily: 'My whole curse stands. There is no chance that I will take it back.'

The king fell silent and returned sadly to the queen, put his arms round her neck and kissed her and again asked her tenderly not to go. The queen said she could not help going, because of his mother's curse; she also said that they might very likely never see one another again, because of the fearful fate that dogged her and the deaths that came to pass through her, these deaths being now so many that the secret would soon be out and she would have to pay the penalty for these crimes, though she had been driven to commit them against her own will.

While she was bewailing her unhappy lot, the shepherd, seeing how matters stood, slipped out of the hall, made his way back across the plain by the shortest route to the cleft, and climbed straight up it. He put the stone of invisibility back in his pocket, put on the bridle, and waited for Queen Hild to come. Shortly afterwards she arrived, and very downcast she was; she seated herself on his back once more, and rode home. When she got there, she gently laid the shepherd on his bed and took the bridle off him, then went to her own bed and lay down to sleep. Although the shepherd had been wide awake all the time, he pretended to be asleep, so that Hild did not realise that he was not. But once she was in bed, he had no need to be on guard, so he fell sound asleep and slept as usual until day.

Next morning the farmer was the first man up, for he was anxious for news of the shepherd; he was preparing himself, not for Christmas joy, but for the grief of finding him dead in bed like his predecessors. So the farmer dressed, roused the others of the house, went to the shepherd's bed, and ran his hands over him. He found then that this shepherd was alive; he rejoiced with his whole heart and thanked God for His mercy. The shepherd woke up, hale and hearty, and dressed; while he was doing so, the farmer asked him whether anything noteworthy had happened to him during the night.

'No,' said the shepherd, 'but I dreamed a very curious dream.'

'What was the dream?' said the farmer.

The shepherd began his story at the point when Hild came to his bed and put the bridle on him, and so went over the whole affair point by point, as well as he could.

When he had ended the tale, all were silent except Hild; she said: 'Everything you have said is a lie, unless you can prove by some good token that it all happened as you said it did.'

The shepherd was not at all put out; he held out the ring which he had found that night on the floor of the hall in Elfland, and said: 'Though I don't hold that I'm bound to prove my dreams true by tokens, I'm quite willing to do so, for I have pretty clear evidence that I was with the elves last night. Isn't this gold ring yours, Queen Hild?'

'It is indeed,' said she, 'and you are a very bold and lucky man, for you have freed me from the bondage that my mother-in-law had laid on me; I had been driven against my will to commit all the crimes she had cursed me with.'

And then Queen Hild told her story, saying: 'I was an elf-girl of low birth, but he who is now King of Elfland fell in love with me, and though it was much against his mother's wishes, he married me. My mother-in-law was so furious that she swore to her son that his time of joy with me would be short, though we might see one another now and then. She laid a curse on me that I was to become a servant in the human world, and added the doom that I would bring death to one man each Christmas by laying my bridle on him as he slept and riding him down the path along which I took this shepherd last night, so as to meet the king. This was to go on until this crime was proved against me and I was put to death, unless I came upon a man so bold and resolute that he would dare follow me to Elfland, and afterwards could prove that he had been there and seen how people live there. Now you can see how all the former shepherds, ever since I came here, met their deaths through me, but I trust I shall not be charged with things done against my own will. Until now, nobody has succeeded in exploring the Lower Road and seeing the elves' homes, except for this valiant man who has set me free from my bondage and the curse. I shall certainly reward him, but later. Now I will stay here no longer, and I thank you for having been good to me. I long now for my own home and my family.'

Having said this, Queen Hild vanished, and she has never been seen again in the world of men.

As for the shepherd, they say he married and built himself a house next spring; the farmer treated him generously when he left, so he had plenty with which to set up house. He became the most prosperous farmer in the district, and people always turned to him for advice and help; indeed, his popularity and credit were hardly credible, and his beasts throve and multiplied, and he himself said he had to thank Queen Hild for all his prosperity.

J.Á. I 110–14. An exclusively Icelandic tale, without exact parallels else-where. Three variants are given by Jón Árnason: that about Una (I 105–7, tr, Powell and Magnússon 80–4), about Ulf-hildur (I 107–10), and about Snotra (I 115–6). The latter heroine is more actively evil, as she challenges each farm bailiff, on pain of death, to discover where she goes. There are also three manuscript variants (Sveinsson 1929). They can all be classified as a sub-type of the international wonder-tale AT 306 'The Danced-Out Shoes', the hero of which wins a human princess by invisibly following her on her nightly visits to the Otherworld, where, it is often stated or implied, she has a non-human lover; proof of her escapade breaks the spell, and she marries the human hero. (AT 507A 'The Monster's Bride' has a similar but more elaborate plot.) The group of Icelandic tales differs radically from the basic prototype in that the heroine belongs by rights to the Otherworld, from which she is exiled by an *álög*-type curse, and the happy ending consists in her permanent return there; the character of her Otherworld husband is correspondingly modified. A similar plot can already be found in the sixteenth-century poem *Snjáskvæ>i*.

AT 306 and 507A both have plots which readily attract motifs based on witchcraft beliefs (see the Icelandic examples classified in Sveinsson 1929 as 306 I, and the discussion of AT 507A by Sven Liljeblad, *Die Tobiasgeschichte*, Lund 1927). In the present instance, Hild's use of a magic bridle (for which see below, pp. 194-5), and the implication that the men found dead in bed on Christmas morning have been ridden to death, derive from the international migratory legend ML 3057*, 'The Witch-Ridden Boy'. This tells of farm servants who are mysteriously exhausted until one, staying awake, lets the farmer's wife turn him into a horse and ride him to a witches' meeting; there, he rids himself of the bridle, and contrives to put it onto the woman herself, turning her into a mare. He rides her home, stopping off on the way at a smithy to have her shod; when he takes the bridle off she becomes a woman again, but the horse-shoes nailed to her hands and feet reveal her crime; the loss of blood breaks her powers, or she is put to death (Simpson 1988, 147; MacDonald, 37; Thorpe 360-1, 606-7). An Icelandic tale of this pattern is given by Jón Árnason (I 440-1, translated in Kvideland and Sehmsdorf 185-7), but its grim conclusion would be inappropriate to Hild, who, like the princess in AT 306, is presented in a romantic and sympathetic light.

The farmer's problems over hiring a shepherd at the beginning of the present tale have parallels in episodes concerning haunted farms in the Family Sagas; the hiring of Glámr in *Grettis saga* is the best-known instance, and may have been the model here.

THE ELVES' DANCE ON NEW YEAR'S EVE

Two brothers once argued over whether the Hidden People existed, one firmly maintaining that they did, while the other obstinately denied it. This went on for some time, till the one who denied the existence of the Hidden People grew angry and said he would leave home and never come back till he was certain whether the Hidden People existed or not. After which he went on his way over hill and dale, mountain and waste land, and was none the wiser.

There is nothing worth telling about his travels until he came, one New Year's Eve, to a farm where all the people were very gloomy. The traveller was curious, and asked what it was that was stopping them from making merry. He was told the reason, which was that nobody dared stay behind and guard the farm while the people there went to the midnight service; since for a long time now anyone who kept guard there on New Year's Eve had vanished, and therefore no one dared stay to guard the farm, for they all thought it would be the death of whoever did so. The newcomer told the men of the household not to let such idle superstitions trouble them, and offered to guard the house himself. At that, their hearts grew lighter, though they were rather afraid of what might happen to him.

As soon as the people of the farm had gone off to church, he set to work and took a plank out of the panelling by the first bed-closet in the main room, and then slipped in there between the panelling and the wall, and then pushed the panelling back into place as much as possible, but left a little crack at the join so that he could see all round the room. But the dog he had with him lay on the floor.

When he had only just finished hiding himself in this way, he heard voices and steps outside, and soon afterwards he hears people coming into the room, and many men come in. He sees his dog picked up and flung down so hard that every bone in its body is broken; next, he hears the strangers saying to one another that there is a smell of human being in the farm, but others say that there is nothing strange in that, since the men of the house had only just set out to church. When the visitors had satisfied their minds on this point, the watcher saw how they set up a table in the room and spread over it a cloth with gold embroidery, a most precious thing, and how everything they laid on the table was made to match – bowls and dishes, goblets and knives, all were of silver. Then they sat down to their meal, where everything was done in the most polished way. These visitors had set a boy to keep watch at the door and see when dawn would break, and he was popping in and out all the time. The human man noticed how each time this lad came in he was asked how time was getting on, but he always replied that there was plenty of time before the day. After this, the watcher began little by little to pull the frame of the door loose, so that he could get away quickly between the panelling and the wall, if need be.

Now when these people had finished eating, he saw a man and woman led forward, and then a third person go up to them who looked to him as if he must be a priest. Some singing began, and the same psalms were sung as always are sung at a marriage service, and everything was done in the same way as among good Christians. As soon as the marriage service was over, dancing began, and this merriment went on for a while.

When the dancing had been going on for some time, the boy who was guarding the door for the Hidden People came in again, and he was asked as before how much of the night was left, and he said there was still one watch.

But at this the human watcher, who had secretly slipped out through the framework of the door and was standing behind the doorkeeper, yelled out, saying: 'You're a liar! There's daylight all over the sky already!'

At this the Hidden People, who were in the middle of their dancing, were so upset that they killed their doorkeeper, and meanwhile the watcher had slipped back between panelling and wall. As soon as the Hidden People had killed their doorkeeper, they rushed out pell-mell like lambs from a fold, and left all their possessions behind. As soon as the human watcher saw this, he chased them a long way, and the last he saw of them was how they flung themselves into a lake a stone's throw from the farm. Then he turned home, and gathered up everything they had left behind, and leftover food and the valuable dishes.

Soon after, the men came back from church, greeted the watchman, and asked whether he had noticed anything; he said there had been a certain amount to see, and told them the whole story. The people of the household felt sure that previous watchers had let themselves be seen, and that that had cost them their lives, just like the dog this time. They thanked the watcher heartily for his action, and gave him everything the Hidden People had left behind, as much as he could carry.

After this he went back home and met his brother; he told him the whole story, and said also that from now on he would never deny that the Hidden People did exist. Later he inherited his parents' farm, married, and was a prosperous man all his life. And as for the farm where he had kept watch, it is said that no man ever disappeared from there again on New Year's Eve.

J.Á. I 123-4. This is ML 6015, 'The Christmas Visitors', a tale that is particularly popular in Norway (Christiansen 1946, 70–87; for an example of the Norwegian versions, see Christiansen 1964, 123–4). It often blends into the international type AT 1161 'The Bear and his Trainer', where a tame bear plays the leading role, for instance in the Swedish examples given in Lindow, 90-1, and in Kvideland and Sehmsdorf, 237–8; the luckless dog in the present version may owe its presence to a confused recollection of that bear. A second Icelandic variant (J.Á. I 118-9, tr. Powell and Magnússon 95–9) is closer to the standard plot of ML 6015 in that the Otherworld intruders, there called 'Sea-Folk', infest the farm on Christmas Eve; a third variant (Maurer 26–7) has the reputed sorcerer fiorleifur fiór>arson (d. 1647) as its hero. The present version elaborates the basic pattern by the framework concerning the two brothers, and by the inset episode of the elfin wedding (another example of interest in the elves' religion).

THE SISTERS AND THE ELVES

There were once two young sisters who lived with their parents, who made the life of one of them a misery, but spoilt the other. One winter night it so happened that everyone on the farm wanted to go to Evensong, and among the rest the girl who was always ill-used very much longed to go, but since someone had to stay behind at home, she was left there, much against her will. And when everybody had gone off, she set to work and cleaned the house from top to bottom and set lamps everywhere, and when she had finished the work she invited the Hidden People into the house with the customary formula: 'Let them come who wish to come, and let them go who wish to go, and do no harm to me or mine.'

After this, she went up into the half-loft and settled down to read her Bible, and never looked up from it till day broke. But as soon as she had sat down, there came into the house a crowd of elves, all dressed in rich clothes and hung about with gold. They laid all kinds of treasures on the floor and offered them to the farmer's daughter; they also started dancing and invited her to join in, but she took no notice, and the elves went on and on like this till dawn. But when dawn broke, the girl looked up at the skylight and said: 'God be praised, dawn has come!' And when the elves heard God's name spoken, they rushed away and left all their treasures behind.

When the people came home, and the girl's sister saw the treasures she had won for herself, she envied her, and said that next year her sister was not to stay at home, for she would stay in herself. So now New Year's Eve comes round again, and the favourite daughter sits at home; she is delighted that the Elfin Folk should come, invites them in, and lights the house up. Then in came the Hidden Folk, just as finely dressed as before, laid their treasures on the floor, began to dance, and invited her to join the dance – and she accepted. But the outcome was that she broke her leg in dancing, and also went out of her mind; but the Hidden People went off, taking all their fine riches with them.

J.Á. I. 124–5; a story current in the West Fjords. For two other tales of girls left alone in the house on Christmas Eve, see J. Á. I 119–20, 120–3. It was long believed in Iceland that elves invaded human homes on both Christmas Eve and New Year's Eve to feast and dance there; on the latter date they might also roam the countryside, as they moved house then. It was therefore the custom to burn lights all over the farmhouse and outbuildings, to leave all doors open, and to sweep the place well; a woman, preferably the mistress of the house, should go round repeating the formula used by the girl in this story; sometimes food was set out for the elves (J.Á. I 105, II 569). These customs are mentioned by Jón Ólafsson of Grunnavík in the first part of the eighteenth century, but are certainly older. Legends attached to these dates stress the risk of being killed or driven mad by the elves, and also often allude to elvish treasures. The present example also incorporates the widespread folktale motif of a moral contrast between sisters and their correspondingly contrasted fates. The group of tales to which this and the preceding two stories belong is discussed by Terry Gunnell, 'The Coming of the Christmas Visitors', forthcoming in *Northern Studies.*

THE ELVES AT THE CROSSROADS

It was once generally believed in Iceland that the Hidden Folk moved house on New Year's Eve, and so one should choose that night to sit at a crossroads and see them go by. They cannot then get past the man at the crossroads, and offer him many treasures, gold and jewels, choice ornaments and delicate foods of every kind. Sometimes elf-women come in the likeness of his mother or sister and urge him to go with them, and all kinds of tricks are tried. If the man stays silent throughout and accepts nothing from them, the jewels and delicacies are left lying near him, and then he can have them, if he holds out till day; but if the man answers or accepts the elves' offers, he is bespelled and loses his wits, and is never in his right mind again.

Some say the right crossroads are those on the fells and moors from which one can see four churches. The oldest belief is that one ought to keep vigil there on Christmas Eve, for that is the real beginning of the New Year, so that to this day Icelanders reckon their age by Christmases, so that, for instance, a boy is said to be fifteen when he has lived through the nights of fifteen Christmas Eves. Later, men changed the date of the beginning of the New Year to the night of 31 December.

There was once a man who sat out at the crossroads one New Year's Eve; some call him Jon, some Fusi, and some do not say what his name was. He sat there all night facing the elves, and no one knew how things were with him until next morning, when he came home and told of what had happened to him. As soon as night fell on the last day of the Old Year, said he, the Hidden Folk began to file past him and offer him gold and silver, fine clothes and costly dishes; for a long while he had spurned all this and remained silent, whatever the offer might be. So the first had gone away, but others had come and done just the same, and they all left behind them whatever they had offered him. This had gone on all night till nearly dawn.

Then, last of all, there came a woman with hot dripping in a ladle (or some say, meat and dripping); but hot dripping was the food Jon liked best of all. And then, so he said, what happened to him was that he looked up and said: 'I don't often say no to dripping.' Through this he lost all the treasures and delicacies that had been offered him and were lying beside him. After this he stood up, and day dawned. From that time on, he lost his mind and wandered in his wits, but still he had the gift of being able to foretell the future from then on, especially because he had already spent whole nights sitting out; it is said he used to prefer to choose the Christmas season for this, for instance Christmas Eve, New Year's Eve,

Epiphany Eve, but also, occasionally, Midwinter Eve and Midsummer Eve. Some say that this Jon was later nicknamed Krukk because of the crossroads, and is the man whose name is so well known in Iceland because of the prophecies attributed to him in manuscripts and oral traditions, known as *Krukksspá*.

A blending of information from J.Á. I 125 and 437. For the very similar belief in divination by summoning the dead at crossroads, see pp. 190–2. The Jón Krukkur mentioned here is a legendary seer alleged to have lived in the early sixteenth century; the 'prophetic' poem *Krukksspá* was attributed to him. He was sometimes thought to be identical with Jón Gu>mundsson the Learned (1574–1658), but this has now been disproved (Sveinsson 2003, 113). For a Norwegian tale embodying the belief that fairies can be seen riding by at crossroads on any of the three nights before Christmas Eve, see Christiansen 1964, 77–8.

THE ELVES MOVE HOUSE

In the first years of the eighteenth century, a farmer named Jon lived at Hvamm in Myrdal. When this story took place, he had many children and was old, and he was living with one of his sons, and his wife with him. To the north of Hvamm there is a ravine, long and deep, which is called Hvammsgil; and east of Hvamm there are two farmsteads called Gotur, and above them a spur of rock which is generally known as Gatnabrun.

One day in autumn when the weather was fine, it so happened that this Jon was standing in the doorway while the people of the house were preparing to go to bed. His wife came up to him and told him to come to bed; he took no notice, but remained staring fixedly towards Gotur, or in that general direction, and while all the rest of the household went to bed, he stood rooted to the spot far into the night.

In the morning he told his wife that just as he had been thinking of coming to bed he happened to look east towards Gotur, and then he saw two men coming down Gatnabrun, and they looked as if they were carrying something very like a lantern between them. They turned into Hvammsgil. Then he saw more and more people coming in groups, men and women too. Some were leading children, others carrying packs, large or small; in short, he saw the moving of all sorts of household goods and, at the end, all sorts of livestock too. The whole company followed the same route as the first two, and it looked very much as if some were carrying torches or lamps in their hands, in the same way as the first. The farmer thought this strange, and so he waited until most of them, if not all, had gone by.

Now the winter that followed that autumn was a terrible one for hard frosts, storms and sleet, mostly coming from the south-west. Households moving house like this one were seen on several other occasions that autumn, but never so many on the move at once. And in the same way next spring, this same farmer, and other men too, saw similar companies moving back again up the same track; and some people were of opinion that the beings who were seen knew beforehand how bad the winter was going to be, and so were moving down into Hvammsgil, possibly from Reynisfjall, to find shelter there. At any rate, one thing is sure – that this did take place, though nobody can say for certain what the explanation may be.

J.Á. I 127–8 (Flutníngurinn), from a story current in Mýrdalur. For another story on this theme, see J.Á. I 126–7, (tr. Craigie 160). Normally, elves were believed to move house at the New Year, unlike human beings, whose moving days were in May; the earliest allusion to a supernatural 'flitting' in Iceland is in fii>randa fláttr ok fiórhalls, when a seer sees all the 'hill-dwellers' moving out, in anticipation of the arrival of Christianity. The 'flitting' of fairies on quarterdays is a fairly common feature in Scottish folklore. The matter-of-fact details given in the present story are typical of the numerous alleged eye-witness accounts of sightings of the Hidden Folk in Iceland.

'MY OLD WOMAN MUST BE PAID'

There was once an old man who lived with his wife in a small cottage; they were so poverty-stricken that they owned nothing of any value at all, except one ball of gold to weight the old woman's spindle. The old man used to go fishing every day to get them something to live on. Not far from their cottage was a large knoll; people believed that this was the home of an elf named Kidhus who was, so they thought, rather light-fingered with other people's belongings. One day, as so often, the old man had gone out fishing and his wife stayed at home as usual. As it was a fine day she sat down out of doors with her spindle, and spun her thread for a while. Now it so happened that the gold weight dropped from the spindle and rolled away, so that she lost sight of it; she was extremely annoyed, and hunted high and low, but all in vain – she could not find her spindle-whorl anywhere.

Afterwards, the old man came home, and she told him all about her misfortune. He said that Kidhus must have taken it, and that this was just like him, and at this he gets ready to go out again, telling the old woman that he means to go to find Kidhus and demand to have it back, or else get something as a fair price for it. At this, the old woman cheers up a little.

So now off goes the old man along the path leading to Kidhus' knoll, and batters it long and hard with his cudgel. At length Kidhus answers:

Who gave my house such a thwack?

The old man says:

Kidhus, it's your neighbour back;
My old woman must be paid
For that weight which she mislaid.

Kidhus asked what he wanted to have in payment for the spindle-whorl, and the old man asked for a cow which would give enough milk at each milking to fill a twenty-eight-pound vat, and Kidhus granted his wish. So the old man went home to his wife with this cow.

Next day, when she had milked the cow night and morning and filled all her pots with milk, it occurred to her that she would make porridge, only then she remembered that she had no oats for the porridge. Then she goes to her husband, and tells him to go and find Kidhus and ask him for porridge-oats.

The old man goes to Kidhus, and batters the knoll, as before. Then says Kidhus:

Who gave my house such a thwack?

The old man says:

Kidhus, it's your neighbour back;
My old woman must be paid
For that weight which she mislaid.

Kidhus asks him what he wants, and the old man asks him to hand out a pot of oats, because he and his wife want to cook themselves some porridge. Kidhus gave the old man a whole barrel of oats. So the old man went home with the barrel, and the old woman makes the porridge.

When the porridge was boiled they sat down to it, the old man and his wife, and ate as much as they possibly could; but when they had eaten till they could eat no more, there was still a lot left in the pot. They began wondering what they could do with the leftovers, and they thought the most profitable plan would be to take them to the Virgin Mary. However, they soon saw it would be rather difficult to jump right up as high as where she was, so they agreed to ask Kidhus for a ladder which would reach up to Heaven, and decided this would not be too much to make up for the spindle-whorl.

The old man goes and batters the knoll where Kidhus lives, and Kidhus asks as before:

Who gave my house such a thwack?

The old man says:

Kidhus, it's your neighbour back;
My old woman must be paid
For that weight which she mislaid.

At that, Kidhus gets a bit annoyed, and says: 'Won't anything ever make up for that damned spindle-whorl?'

The old man begged and prayed, saying he wanted to take his leftover porridge to the Virgin Mary in a pail. Kidhus let himself be talked into it, gave him the ladder, and set it upright for him. Then the old man was very glad, and went home to his wife.

They got ready for the journey, taking the pail of porridge with them. But when they had gone a good long way up the ladder their heads began to swim, and this upset them so much that they both came tumbling down and cracked their skulls open. Splashes of brains and lumps of porridge went flying all over the place. Wherever the bits of their brains touched the rocks they turned into white lichen, and the lumps of porridge into yellow lichen, and both of these can be seen on rocks to this day.

J.Á. II 508–9 ('*Kerling vill hafa nokku> fyrir snú> sinn*'), from Sigur>ur Gu>mundsson (d.1874). A variant of AT 555, 'The Fisherman and his Wife', but one in which the initial motive-force is no longer a supernatural being's gratitude but a human being's demand for compensation for an injury – a concept very familiar from the sagas. Moreover, a stupid old man and wife are stock figures in Icelandic numskull tales; their wish to give a present to the Virgin is paralleled in an Icelandic variant of AT 1435* (Rittershaus 359), and their fall from the ladder in the Slavonic AT 804A, 'The Beanstalk to Heaven'. Beating an elf's knoll is also mentioned in some Danish tales as a method of obtaining magic gifts from him.

2

TROLLS

Blessing the Cliffs

Until the latter part of the nineteenth century there was an evil spirit in a cave on Grimsey Island. Whenever the men there used to let themselves down over the edge of the cliff to catch seabirds, a shaggy grey hand would come out of the cliff and cut the rope, and so kill the men who hung from it. In the end Parson Pall Tomasson blessed the cliff – or so say the people of Grimsey. This priest Pall had noticed that there were sharp ridges jutting from the cliff, against which ropes would fray; so he got the men of Grimsey to tie a rope round him and went down the cliff-face, but before he went down he had stuck a hammer in his jacket without the local people seeing it. And he gave them the task of singing psalms as loud as they could all the while he was down the cliff-face, and never to let there be a moment's silence until he gave them the signal to draw him up. As a result of this device the inhabitants of the island thought that their priest Pall had blessed the cliff, whereas he had made them sing so that they would hear nothing while he used his hammer to chip away the sharp ridges from the cliff; and since then no men have been killed on the ropes at that spot.

Stories about blessing cliffs were very common in the past, and were ascribed to the days of Bishop Thorlak the Saint, who died in 1193, and of Bishop Gudmund the Good, who died in 1237. Bishop Thorlak is supposed to have blessed several cliffs where seabirds nest, and to have driven evil spirits out of them. When he blessed Latrabjarg in the west country, he heard a voice say from the cliff, in words which have since become a proverb, 'The wicked do have to have somewhere to live.' Then the bishop left a small area of the cliff unblessed, and no one ever dared go down a rope there. Even so, one fool of a man did do so, once; then there came a grey hand out of the cliff, and it cut the rope, and that man met with a sudden death.

Others say that it was Bishop Gudmund who blessed Latrabjarg when he was wandering homeless round the west, and that when he had gone a great way in blessing it, somebody inside the cliff said: 'I beg you to go no further, Bishop, for in the face of your prayers and ceremonies we are forced to flee, yet the wicked do have to have somewhere to live.' It is said that the bishop did stop, and that afterwards it was his custom when blessing such cliffs to leave some part of them unblessed.

Those parts of nesting-cliffs which are said never to have been blessed are commonly called 'Heathen Cliff', and this name is found in many places; it is thought dangerous to go down them, and nobody ever does. In some cases it is elves, not trolls, that are thought to live there.

J.Á. I 143–4; cf. Maurer 40–1. A legend partially resembling this one is to be found in a collection of miracles attributed to Bishop Gu>mundr Arason the Good, compiled early in the fourteenth century. A certain Eiríkr Árnason went gathering birds' eggs on a cliff which was reputed dangerous before mid-morning and after mid-evening; he lingered there too late, and as he began to climb back up the cliff-face, a hand came out of the rock and began cutting through his rope; eight strands parted, but the ninth, which had been blessed by Bishop Gu>mundr, held firm and saved his life (*Byskupa sögur*, ed. G. Jónsson, 1948, II 484). In a later local legend, the Bishop himself is said to have been in peril of his life when, as he hung on a rope against a cliff-face to bless it, a huge grey paw in a red sleeve emerged and began to cut the rope; two strands parted, but the third held, having been particularly well blessed, and so the troll desisted, and merely begged the Bishop to leave him space to live, in the traditional words (J.Á. I 144–6). Jón Árnason names several cliffs known as 'heathen cliffs' and shunned by fowlers; some are held to have been homes of elves or 'spirits of the land' rather than of trolls (J.Á. I 144).

The Revd Páll Tómasson, resourceful hero of the first part of this story, died in 1881; he was a colourful personality, about whom several anecdotes have been preserved.

THE OGRESS OF MJOAFJORD

Out beyond the farm called Fjord in Mjoafjord, there is a ravine known as Mjoafjord Ghyll. At one time an ogress lived there, and she was in the habit of putting a spell on the priests at Fjord and so drawing them to her in the ravine. This was how she did it: she would go up to the church as soon as the priest had gone into the pulpit and would hold up her hand outside the window nearest the pulpit, and then the priests would go mad and say:

> *You can pluck out my guts and groin,*
> *To the Ghyll I long to go;*
> *You can pluck out my spleen and loin,*
> *But to Mjoafjord Ghyll I go.*

Having said this, they would rush out of church and off to the Ghyll, and that was the last anyone ever heard of them.

One day a traveller was passing through the ravine and saw the ogress high up above him, sitting on a jutting rock of the cliff, and holding something in her hand.

He called out to her, and said: 'What are you holding there, old woman?'

'I'm just gnawing the last bits off the skull of that Parson Snjoki,' said the ogress.

The man spread the news, and it was not thought good news.

Many priests there went the same way, one after another, and this became rather a problem, because priests grew unwilling to go to Fjord when they learnt what a deadly monster there was in the ravine. In the end there came a time when no one would go there at all, but then a certain priest offered to go there himself, though he knew quite well what a fearful creature there was in the ravine. Before he said Mass at Fjord for the first time, he took the precaution of telling his parish-

ioners what they must do if they saw anything wild come over him in
the pulpit; he ordered that six men should rush at him and hold him
down, another six run to the church bells and ring them, and ten run
to the door. He chose the men to do this, and said what each must do.

As soon as the priest had gone up into the pulpit, the hand
appeared at the window and waved about outside; then the priest
went mad and said:

> *You can pluck out my guts and groin,*
> *To the Ghyll I long to go;*
> *You can pluck out my spleen and loin,*
> *But to Mjoafjord Ghyll I go.*

The priest then tried to go out, but the six men who had been told
to do so sprang on him, and the other six rang the bells, and the ten
ran to the door. As soon as the ogress heard the bells she took to her
heels; she jumped onto the churchyard wall, and a great gap opened
up in it under her feet, and at that she said: 'May you never stand
again!' The ogress ran off into the ravine, and that was the last anyone
has ever seen of her. But as for the gap where the ogress trod the wall
down, however well one builds it up again, it never holds together.

J.Á. I 152–3, from Þórarinn Jónsson (d.1865). For two other tales of canni-
balistic she-trolls, see J.Á. I 153–6 (tr. Powell and Magnússon 122–4,
124–31; Craigie 48–50); yet another, who tried to carry off Bishop
Brynjólfur of Skalholt (d.1675), was converted by him, and thereafter stole
only horses for her Christmas meal (J.Á. I 159–60). The horror evil giants
feel at the sound of church bells is a common feature in troll-tales; sometimes they even turn to stone at the sound. Common, too, is the unfillable
gap in a churchyard wall which the legend attempts to explain; often it is
ascribed to a giantess' curse (J.Á. I 156, 188, 191, 195), or sometimes to the
kick of a Water-Horse (J.Á. I xix, 137, 518; cf. p.113). One of the owners of
the farm to which the present tale is attached, who died around 1830,
remembered seeing an iron trug used there for carrying refuse, which was
believed to have been the ogress' shoe, fallen off when she kicked the wall.

SOME SHE-TROLLS

It is said that at one time the Eskifjord Dales began to be haunted by trolls, and this grew worse and worse, and so much damage was done that no one thought it safe to move about except in large groups, and in broad daylight. It happened once that six men were travelling home from market together up Eskifjord, following the road through the valley, and it was almost dusk. They saw pitch-black clouds gathering over the mountain called Skagafell north of the valley, and these clouds towered up higher and higher till in the end they seemed to take on human shape, and then they heard a frightful voice calling out so loud that it boomed among the mountains on every side, and it said: 'Hey there, hey, sister!'

Then they heard a second call from behind them, answering: 'Oh hey there, sister, hey!'

At this they looked round, and saw a second monstrous shape on the other side of the valley, standing on the mountain known as Slenjudalsfjall.

They heard the first speak again: 'What's up, sister?'

Then the second answered: 'The shieling has been given to someone.'

'Who to?' says the first.

The second answers: 'To that mouldy-headed Jon of Vallaness!'

Then the first says : 'Let's fly then, sister, fly!'

'Where to?' answers the second.

'To Blaskogar,' says the other.

After that they disappeared from the sight of the travellers, and from that time the hauntings also decreased, because the shieling up on Tunga had been given to Parson Jon who was priest at Vallaness, and he had been asked to drive the evil creatures away, and people thought they had been uprooted pretty quick.

Now that the haunting had stopped in the Eskifjord Dales, people began to notice that there were trolls about in Blaskogar, in the south; men did not dare pass that way, and so that road fell into disuse, though it had been much used before. When this had been going on for two or three years, it so happened that the men of Thingey lost count of the date, and did not know when Christmas Day would fall. So they decided to send a man south to Skalholt to get a ruling from the Bishop to clear up this problem.

The man chosen to make the journey was called Olaf, and he was a bold and resourceful man. He went up into the mountains from Bardardal, and so south by way of Spreingisand, and reached Blaskogar late in the day. He did not want to loiter there, so he pressed on, and when it was almost dusk he saw a fearsome great she-troll standing on the mountain called Blafell, which is very near the road. This she-troll called out in a rumbling voice, saying:

> *You going south,*
> *Olaf Big-Mouth?*
> *Twisted-Gob, I tell you plain*
> *You'd better go straight home again!*
> *Wipe your snotty little face,*
> *And snuffle off to your own place!*

Then he said:

> *Hail to you! I wish you well,*
> *Lady Hallgerd of Blafell!*

Then she roared back:

> *Such kind words I seldom hear;*
> *Fare you well, my darling dear!*

There's nothing more to tell about his journey till he came to Skalholt, where he got the solution to his problem, and having fulfilled his errand he set off home again by the same road. As soon as he came to Blaskogar, the she-troll was there to meet him, and it seemed to him that she was not so horrible-looking as he remembered. She handed him what has since been known as the She-Troll's Calendar, and said: 'If Christ the son of Mary had done as much for us trolls as you say He has done for you men, we would not have forgotten the date of His birthday.'

When she had said this, they parted, and after that there were no more hauntings in Blaskogar. Olaf went back north, and men thought he had behaved cleverly, but from then on he was known as Olaf Big-Mouth.

J.Á. I 156–8 (*Gellivör*, final sections), from Sæbjörn Egilsson (b.1836). For other examples of conversations between mountain trolls, see the next tale and its note. The story of Ólafur Big-Mouth and the she-troll, with its associated verse, is given in two more versions (J.Á. I 158–9); in the first they part friends, as here, but in the second he tricks her into looking at the sunrise, so that she is turned to stone. These versions do not include the detail that Ólafur was wanting to learn when Christmas Day was due – a motif known in Norway, with reference to people isolated by the Black Death (ML 6030, 'The Message of the Fairies'; for an example, see Christiansen 1964, 127–8).

THE SHEPHERDESS AND THE TROLLS

It happened in the west of Iceland, in Dalasysla, that a young shepherdess went to church to Communion. As soon as she got back from church she went straight out to her sheep, without giving herself time to sit down and eat.

As she was going along past certain crags, she hears a voice coming from one of them: 'Hey, Ragnhild of the Red Rocks!'

From another crag came the answer: 'What do you want, Ogre of the Three Rocks?'

Then says he: 'Here's a nice bit of meat running up the road. Let's take her, let's take her!'

Then from the other crags the answer came: 'No, let her go by, shame on her! Her mouth is all smeared with coal!'

The girl went on her way, and heard no more talk from this troll and his wife.

J.Á. I 160 (*Smalastúlkan*), from a schoolboy in Western Iceland, 1845. The alleged dirt is of course simply the troll's inverted perception of the protective holiness conferred by Communion. A very similar story is told about a certain Gissur: one day, returning from taking Communion, he heard one she-troll shout to another: 'Sister, lend me a pot.' – 'Better not. To do what?' – 'To boil a man.' – 'Who's the one?' – 'Gissur of Botn, Gissur of Lækjarbotn.' – 'You won't get him, he's grubby round the jaws.' (J.Á. I 163–4). The rhymed and rhythmic part of the dialogue occurs also in a variant without the Communion motif (J.Á. I 161–2), and has close parallels in the Norwegian ML 5000, 'Trolls Resent a Disturbance' (see Christiansen 1964, 81-2, 143). Similarly in a Swedish tale two trolls are heard shouting to each other about how they will cook a man who has been stealing fish from a mountain lake (Kvideland and Sehmsdorf, 304-5).

THE OLD MAN OF THE CLIFF

Once when King Olaf Tryggvason was on board a ship at the foot of a certain cliff, and his men with him, it happened that an old man appeared on the cliff and hailed the king and his men. The king asked him where his home might be, to which the old man replied that his dwelling was inside this very cliff. Then the king asked him how many men he had at his command, whereupon the old man answered in these words:

> *Twelve boats have I off shore;*
> *In every boat there are twelve men;*
> *And every man, he kills twelve seals;*
> *Into twelve strips each seal is flayed;*
> *Into twelve lengths each strip is cut;*
> *Two men sit down to share each piece –*
> *Work it out yourself, O king!*

While the king was reckoning it all up, the old man's wizardry was drawing the ship backwards into the inside of the cliff, during the time the king was kept busy reckoning up how large a household the old man kept.

Seeing that they were in this desperate plight, a certain Thorgeir, who was one of the king's men on board, snatched up the sailyard and set one end of it against the cliff and the other against his own chest. The trollish magic of the old man was drawing the ship in, but Thorgeir stood firm against it. He taxed his strength so severely that at last his breastbone and his lower ribs snapped, but at that very moment the ship shot away from the cliff and out to sea, for it was freed from the spell. From this exploit of his, Thorgeir got his nickname 'Punt-Pole-Head'.

J.Á. I 164–5 (*Saga af* fi *orgeiri stjakarhöf>a*), from a written account by Árni Magnússon (d.1730), who had heard the tale told by his uncle Vigfúss Jónsson (d.1728). Óláfr Tryggvason ruled Norway from 995 to 1000, and already in the earliest saga about him (a Latin work by Oddr Snorrason, *c*.1190) several episodes concerned his encounters with heathen gods in human guise, or with malevolent trolls. The present tale follows a pattern already visible in two of Oddr's episodes, in that it shows the king put off guard by a riddle just as, in the early work, he was beguiled by Ó>inn's tales of ancient heroes and by the jokes of fi órr.

GILITRUTT

O nce there was a young farmer living out in the east, at the foot of Eyjafjoll; he was a most energetic, hard-working man. There was good grazing round where he lived, and he had many sheep. He had recently married at the time when this story takes place. His wife was young, but lazy and good-for-nothing; she had no liking for work of any kind, and took little part in running the farm. Her husband was very annoyed about it, but there was nothing he could do.

One autumn he brought her a lot of wool, and told her to make it up into cloth in the course of the winter, but she was in no hurry to set about it. So the winter wore on and the young woman never touched the wool, though the farmer often made a point of mentioning it.

One day some old woman, rather massively built, comes to the farmer's wife and asks her to give her a little help.

'Could you do some work for me in return?' says the wife.

'Very good,' says the old woman, 'and what am I to work at?'

'Make some wool up into cloth,' says she.

'Give it me, then,' says the old woman.

The farmer's wife picks up a huge great sack of wool and gives it to her.

The old woman takes hold of the sack, slings it over her shoulder, and says: 'I'll come back with the cloth on the first day of summer.'

'What payment will you want?' says the wife.

'Nothing much,' says the old woman. 'You must tell me my name in three guesses, and then we'll be quits.'

She agreed, and now the old woman goes off.

Now the winter wears on, and the farmer often asks her where the wool is, but she tells him not to worry over that, and that he'll get it on the first day of summer. The farmer showed that he was none too pleased, and so time went by and winter was drawing to a close. Then the farmer's wife starts wondering about the old woman's name, but she can't see any way to discover it, and she grew very anxious and miserable about it. The farmer sees how she has changed, and asks her to tell him what was the matter with her. She then told him the whole story. Then the farmer grew frightened, and says that she has done wrong, for this must be a troll which meant to carry her off.

One day after this, the farmer had to go up into the mountains, and came upon a large cave. He was thinking of his troubles, and hardly knew where he was. Then he hears the sound of heavy blows inside the cave; he goes nearer to listen, comes upon a peep-hole, and there he sees a woman of massive size sitting weaving. She has the web between her legs and is thumping it heartily.

She muttered between her teeth: 'Ha ha, ho ho! The housewife doesn't know what my name is, ha ha and ho ho! My name's Gilitrutt, ha ha and ho ho! My name's Gilitrutt, ha ha and ho ho!'

She went on and on like this, and thumped the web vigorously. The farmer was glad, and felt sure that this must be the old woman who had visited his wife in the autumn. So then he goes home and writes down a note of the name Gilitrutt, but does not tell his wife about it.

Now 24 April, the last day of winter, had come; the housewife was wretched, and would not even dress that day. Then the farmer comes to her and asks whether she knows the name of the woman working for her. She said no, and that she thought her heart would break. The farmer said there was no need for that, handed her the paper with the name on it, and told her the whole story. She took the paper, shaking with terror, she was so afraid the name might be wrong. She asks her husband to be with her when the old woman comes, but he says: 'No, you acted on your own when you gave her the wool, so you had better settle the payment alone.' Then off he goes.

Now the first day of summer comes, and the housewife was lying alone in her bed, and there was nobody else in the house. She then hears a great din and a rumbling noise, and in comes the old woman, and she looks far from pleasant now. She flings a huge roll of cloth across the floor, and says: 'Now then, what's my name? What's my name?'

The wife, more dead than alive with fright, says: 'Signy?'

'That's my name, is it? That's my name, is it? Guess again, mistress!' says the old woman.

'Asa?' says she.

'That's my name, is it? That's my name, is it? Guess again, mistress!'

'I don't suppose,' says she then, 'that your name is Gilitrutt?'

The old woman was so startled that she fell flat on her bum on the floor, and a mighty crash that was! Then she got up and went off, and was never seen again. The farmer's wife was happier than I can say that she was lucky enough to give this monster the slip, and from now on she was quite a different person; she became hard-working, ran her house properly, and from then on always wove her own wool.

J.Á. I 181–2, from an old woman in Rángárfling. A variant of the international AT 500, 'The Name of the Helper', 'Rumplestiltskin' or 'Tom Tit Tot', though lacking the normal opening. Another version, further from the prototype and showing French influence, is in J.Á. II 20–2; there are also two loosely related unpublished versions (Sveinsson 1929, 59–60), one of which is much closer to the 'Church-Builder' legend (see pp.48–9, above).

How Kraka Lost her Lover

In the old days a giantess whose name was Kraka had her home in Blahvamm by Blafjall; she lived in a cave which is still to be seen, and it is so high among the crags that it is impossible for any human being to reach it. Kraka was a most pernicious creature; she took a heavy toll of the cattle of the Myvatn men and did them great harm by carrying cattle off and killing people. Kraka was also man-mad, and could not bear to live alone; it was by no means unusual for her to carry men off from their homes and keep them with her, but there were few who would agree to make love to her rather than run away or kill themselves.

It happened once that Kraka got hold of a shepherd from the farm Baldursheim, whose name was Jon. She took him home to her cave and wanted to make a very fine feast for him, but he proved hard to please and refused to touch anything Kraka set before him; she tried every trick she knew to find something which would take his fancy, but there was nothing doing. Finally, the shepherd said that he would get his appetite back if he could have a twelve-year-old shark to eat. Now Kraka knew, through her magic powers, that there was nowhere one could catch a twelve-year-old shark except off

Siglunes, and though it was a terrible long way from Blahvamm, she wants all the same to try and see if she can catch this shark.

So she sets out, leaving the shepherd behind, but when she has gone only a little way it strikes her that it would be wiser to see whether the shepherd hasn't tricked her and run off while her back was turned. Then she runs back home to her cave, and the shepherd is quite quiet. So off she goes again, and gets rather further than the first time; then she is gripped by the same fear as before that the shepherd will not prove faithful to her, and so Kraka runs back home to her cave, but the shepherd is quiet, just as before. Therefore she sets out once again, thinking that there is no need now to distrust the shepherd, and she makes a beeline for Siglunes, wading straight out across Eyjafjord north of Hrisey Isle. There is no more to say about her journey, except that she was lucky enough to catch the shark, and took the same road home again.

As for the shepherd, as soon as he thinks Kraka must have gone right away, he takes to his heels and runs; but before he had been long gone, back comes Kraka, and very soon realises that her shepherd has disappeared. She sets out at full speed in pursuit, and when the shepherd is almost home again in Baldursheim he hears a great crashing and banging behind him, and knows what it must be – it must be Kraka coming. And when she is near enough for him to hear her voice, she calls out: 'Here's the shark, Jon! It's a twelve-year-old – thirteen, in fact!'

But he takes no notice; and as he reaches the farm, the farmer is working in his smithy. The shepherd runs into the smithy, straight up to the farmer, and at that very moment Kraka reaches the smithy door. The farmer snatches a mass of red-hot iron from the hearth and runs towards Kraka, saying he will ram it into her if she doesn't turn back, and also promise never to bother him or his men again. Kraka saw she had no choice but to turn back, and so she did. It is said that she never molested the farmer of Baldursheim after this.

J.Á. I 186–7 (*Kráka tröllskessa*), from Jón Sigur>sson á Gautlöndum, Member of the Alflingi (d. 1889). Jón Árnason gives several more anecdotes about

Kráka (I 188–9), two of which concern other unsuccessful attempts at amorous abduction; there follow four other similar stories about other giantesses (I 189–95; one tr. Powell and Magnússon 135–8, another in Craigie 54–6), and there is another in Maurer, p. 47, It is sometimes made clear that the abducted man would slowly turn into a troll himself if he stayed with the giantess and ate her food; one tale describes how two ogresses rub their captive with ointment, stretch him, and bellow into his ear, in an attempt to make a troll of him. Flight from an amorous supernatural being is also the theme of certain Norwegian tales (ML 5095, 'Fairy Woman Pursues Man'); there the hero, having almost been seduced by an elf-woman when alone in the mountains, realises what she is and flees, stealing her own skis to do so, and hotly pursued by her (cf. Christiansen 1964, 128–9).

In the Icelandic tales, the amorous she-troll is normally foiled by the ringing of church bells; the part played here (and in Maurer's version) by the farmer at his smithy recalls the myth of fiórr slaying a giant by hurling a mass of glowing iron at him. Kráka's journey from near Mývatn to Siglunes is over seventy miles as the crow flies, crossing mountains and wading through Eyjafjör>ur at almost its broadest point.

TRUNT, TRUNT, AND THE TROLLS IN THE FELLS

There were once two men who went up into the mountains to gather edible moss. One night they were sharing a tent, and one was asleep but the other awake. The one who was awake saw the one who was asleep go creeping out; he got up and followed him, but however hard he ran he could not catch up with him. The sleeping man was heading straight up the mountain towards the glaciers, and the other saw where a huge giantess was sitting up there on a spur of the glacier. What she was doing was this: she would stretch out her arms with her hands crossed and then draw them in again to her breast, and in this way she was magically drawing the man towards her. The man ran straight into her arms, and she then ran off with him.

A year later, some people from this man's district were gathering moss at the same place; he came there to meet them, and he was so short-spoken and surly that one could hardly get a word out of him. They asked him who he believed in, and he said he believed in God. The following year he came to the moss-gatherers again, and by then he looked so like a troll that he struck terror into them. However, he was again asked who he believed in, but he made no reply. This time he stayed a shorter time with them than before. The third year, he came again; by then he had turned into an absolute troll, and a very ugly-looking one too. Yet someone plucked up courage to ask him who he believed in, but he said he believed in 'Trunt, Trunt, and the trolls in the fells' – and then he disappeared. After this he was never seen again, but for some years afterwards men did not dare go looking for moss in that place.

J.Á. I 193, from the Revd Skúli Gíslason (d. 1888), from a story current in Northern Iceland. Here the amorous ogress is a more sinister figure, and the progressive degeneration of her victim is taken more seriously. Comparable tales were current in Sweden about the *skogsrå*, a forest spirit who was much dreaded for her power to lure men to her, seduce them, and sometimes drive them mad (von Sydow 1931, 123–4; Lindow 36–7, 105–14).

The word 'Trunt' is nonsensical, unless perhaps it is a corruption of 'Trond', the name of the king of the trolls in some Norwegian versions of ML 6015, 'The Christmas Visitors'.

THE BALLADS OF ANDRI
AND THE HYMNS OF HALLGRIM

Some fishermen from northern Iceland were once travelling overland to the south, and were caught in a very bad storm among the mountains, so that they lost their way and had no idea where they were going. In the end they came on a cleft in the rock opening into a cave, and went far enough in to be out of reach of the wind and the driving rain. There they stayed for shelter, struck a light, and made a fire with moss which they stripped from the rocks, and so began to warm up and get their strength back.

Now these men began to discuss what they could do to pass the time enjoyably; some wanted to recite the 'Ballads of Andri', but others to sing Parson Hallgrim's 'Passion Hymns'. Deeper in from where they were they saw a shadowy cleft, as if a new twist in the cave led off from there. Then they heard a voice in there in the darkness, saying:

> *The Andri Ballads I like best,*
> *The Hallgrim Ballads I detest.*

So then they started reciting the 'Ballads of Andri' as long and as loud as they could; the one who recited best was called Bjorn. This went on far into the evening.

Then the voice in there in the darkness said: 'Now I enjoyed that, but my wife didn't; she wants to hear Hallgrim's Ballads.'

Then the men started singing the hymns, but soon got to the end of all the verses they knew.

Then the voice said: 'Now my wife enjoyed that, but I didn't.' And then it said: 'You, Bjorn the Reciter, would you like to lick the inside of my ladle as your reward?'

He said he would, so then a large tub fixed to a handle was thrust out, with porridge in it, and all of them together could hardly cope with this ladle. The porridge was good and pleasant to eat; three of them ate some, and it did them no harm, but one of them did not dare. Then they lay down to sleep, and slept long and soundly.

Next day they went to take a look at the weather, and it was clear and bright. Now they wanted to be on their way again, but the man who had not dared eat the night before was so fast asleep that he could not be woken.

Then one said: 'It's better to kill a comrade than to leave him like this, in the hands of trolls.'

With that, he punched him on the nose so that blood gushed out all over him, and at that he woke up and so escaped with his companions, and after this they reached human dwellings safe and sound. People maintain that this troll must have enticed some woman of the district to him by magic, and that the fishermen owed their lives to her.

J.Á. I 196, from the Revd Skúli Gíslason, from a story current in Northern Iceland. A variant, attached to an islet in Rei>arfjör>ur, tells how fishermen who sang hymns in honour of the Virgin Mary got porridge, while others who sang the *Andrarímur* got hot mutton and dripping (J.Á. I 196–7, tr. Powell and Magnússon 138–40; see also J.Á. I 162–3 for a simpler variant, omitting the troll's wife and having the secular song only). The choice between the *Andrarímur* and 'Hallgrim's Hymns' is roughly equivalent to one between, say, the Robin Hood ballads and the hymns of Charles Wesley. The former tells of the highly entertaining and fantastic adventures of a certain Earl Andri, himself half a troll; the latter, the 'Passion Hymns' by the Revd Hallgrímur Pétursson (d.1674), are among the best loved Icelandic hymns. By calling them 'Hallgrim's Ballads' the troll is revealing his barbarous heathen prejudice.

Despite the common folktale taboo on eating food from supernatural beings, there are also examples of the opposite idea that to refuse it is rude and dangerous; cf. ML 5080, 'Food from the Fairies', in which a boy who takes it grows strong, but another who will not do so falls ill. For disenchantment by drawing blood by a blow on the nose, cf. the stories about catching elfin cows and sea-cows (pp.37–9, 108–9), and also the widespread belief that a witch's power will leave her if she is scratched 'above the breath'.

THE NIGHT-TROLL

On a certain farm, whoever stayed at home to mind the house on Christmas Eve while the others were at Evensong used to be found next morning either dead or out of his mind. The servants there thought this very bad, and few wanted to be the one to stay at home on Christmas Eve. On one occasion a young girl offered to mind the farm; the others were delighted, and went off. The girl sat in the main room, and sang to a child which she held in her arms.

During the course of the night someone comes to the window, and says:

> *Fair seems your hand to me,*
> *Hard and rough mine must be,*
> *Dilly-dilly-do.*

Then says she:

> *Dirt did it never sweep,*
> *Sleep, little Kari, sleep,*
> *Lully-lully-lo.*

Then the voice at the window says:

> *Fair seem your eyes to me,*
> *Hard and rough mine must be,*
> *Dilly-dilly-do.*

Then says she:

> *Evil they never saw,*
> *Sleep, Kari, sleep once more,*
> *Lully-lully-lo.*

Then the voice at the window says:

> *Fair seem your feet to me,*
> *Hard and rough mine must be,*
> *Dilly-dilly-do.*

Then says she:

> *Dirt did they never crush,*
> *Hush, little Kari, hush,*
> *Lully-lully-lo.*

Then the voice at the window says:

Day in the east I see,
Hard and rough mine must be,
Dilly-dilly-do.

Then says she:

Stand there and turn to stone,
So you'll do harm to none,
Lully-lully-lo.

Then the uncanny creature vanished from the window. But in the morning when the people came home, a huge stone had appeared in the path between the farm buildings, and it has stood there ever since. Then the girl spoke of what she had heard – but she had seen nothing, for she never once looked round – and it must have been a Night-Troll which had come to the window.

J.Á. I 208–9, from an old woman in Rángárfling. 'Night trolls' are a particular type of troll who cannot bear daylight, for it turns them to stone. They are often associated with particular rocks, either as having been turned into them, or as living in them, or as buried under them; some are said to be malevolent, others harmless (J.Á. I 207–8). Many tales of encounters with ghosts and devils stress the need for skill in impromptu versifying, and the vital necessity of getting the last word; those who cannot cap the evil creature's verse by another in the same metre will go mad or be carried off, but those who can will put it to flight (J.Á. I 463–5; cf. Briggs 1971, I 534–5, 567). The present story gives yet another example of an uncanny visitant haunting a farmstead on Christmas Eve.

THE ORIGIN OF DRANGEY ISLAND

In the old days there were two Night-Trolls living on Hegranes, an old man and his wife; there is nothing much to say about them until one day when it happened that their cow was in heat, and then (whether because they had no one to send, or because they thought that if you want something well done you had best do it yourself) they set off to lead the cow to a bull themselves, so that she should not miss her time. The old man led the cow by a rope, and the old woman drove her from behind, as the custom is.

So along they went with the cow, out over Hegranes and a good way out into the waters of Skagafjord; but when they still had quite a distance to go before they were half way across, they saw the first gleam of day on the east side of the fjord, shining on the rock slopes and over the crests of the fells. And since it is sudden death to Night-Trolls if dawn catches them, this daylight cost them their lives, and they each turned into a stack of rock; these are the stacks which stand there now, one on the seaward side of Drangey, which is the old man, and one on the landward side, which is the old woman. These rock stacks take their names from this, and are called The Old Man and The Old Woman to this day. And as for the cow, she was turned into the island itself, and though history does not relate whether she had occasion to be got with calf in the course of her travels with the trolls, she certainly proved fertile land for the men of Skagafjord.

J.Á. I 210; a tale current round Skagafjör>ur and Húnavatn. For other tales about off-shore rocks being trolls turned to stone, see J.Á. I 209–11. There are Scottish and Faroese parallels, for instance about two huge rock-stacks called Risin and Kellingin ('Giant' and 'Old Woman') to the north of Streymoy (Williamson, 261). Inland rock-formations may be explained by similar legends (J.Á. I 214–7).

Jón Árnason adds that in his own time there was a custom that every man sailing out to Drangey for the first time in the year must greet the island itself and its two rock stacks, saying to each: 'Hail and good luck to you, and to all your spirits!' It was largely kept up as a joke, but must have originated in the ancient belief, well exemplified in medieval sagas and laws, that every part of the land had its guardian nature-spirits.

BERGTHOR OF BLAFELL

There was a man named Bergthor who lived in a cave on Blafell; his wife's name was Hrefna. His father was Thorolf of Thorolfsfell, who was also known as Kalfstindar, and his mother was called Hladgerd, and she lived in Hlodkufell. The land was still heathen in the days when all this took place, and it was in the days of the she-troll Hit, after whom Hitardal takes its name. Bergthor was one of her guests when she invited all the trolls in the country to a feast in Hundahellir Cave; after the meal Hit asked the trolls to find some way of enjoying themselves, and they chose tests of strength, and Bergthor was always judged the strongest. Bergthor would not harm human beings, provided nothing was done to annoy him, and he was believed to have the gift of foresight, and great wisdom.

After the country became Christian, Hrefna thought Blafell an unpleasant place, since from there she looked out over Christian farmlands. These new ways were so little to her liking that she wanted to move house with her husband, northwards to the other side of Hvita River; but Bergthor said his countrymen's change of religion did not bother him, and he meant to stay quietly in his cave. Hrefna stuck to her own opinion, and moved house north across the river; there she built herself a hall at the foot of the mountain, and the spot has been called Hrefna's Booth ever since. After this, she and Bergthor only met when they were both fishing for trout in Hvita Lake.

Bergthor would often go down to Eyrarbakki to buy meal, especially in winter when the lake was frozen over, and he always carried back two full barrels of meal. Once Bergthor was going home through the cultivated regions with his load, and as he comes up to the homefield of Bergstadir Farm, he meets the farmer and asks him to give him a drink. Bergthor says he'll wait while the farmer goes back to the house to fetch the drink, so he sets his load down at the foot of the mountain from which the farm takes its name, and chips out a hollow in the rock with the iron spike of his staff. The farmer comes back with the drink and gives it to Bergthor, who drinks his fill, thanks him, and tells him that he must use the hollow he has chipped in the rock as a vat to keep sour whey in; he says that no water will ever mix with the whey in that vat, nor will the whey freeze in it in winter – but that if the farmer refused to use it, innumerable misfortunes would come upon his household. Having said all this, Bergthor bade the farmer farewell, and went on his way.

Bergthor once came to talk with a farmer in Haukadal when he had grown very old. He says he wants to choose himself a place for his grave, somewhere from which one can hear church bells and prayers, and so he asks this man to fetch his dead body down to Haukadal, and tells him that for his trouble he can take what there will be in a cauldron by his bed, and that as soon as he is dead there will be a token for the farmer, namely that his staff will be outside the farm door. The farmer promises to do this, and so they part.

Time passes and passes, and there is no news of Bergthor, up until one morning when the people of Haukadal come downstairs and there, in front of the farm door, is a huge great walking-staff. The men bring word of this to the farmer; he says little, but goes out, and sees that it is indeed Bergthor's staff. He gives orders for a large coffin to be made at once, and sets out northwards for Blafell with several men.

There is nothing to tell about their journey until they reach Bergthor's cave away in the north; there they see Bergthor dead in his bed, lay him in the coffin, and think that he is remarkably light for his size. Now the farmer sees a large cauldron by the bed; he looks to see what there is in it and sees nothing but leaves inside, so he thinks Bergthor must have been mocking him, and never gives it a second thought. But one of his companions fills both his gloves with the leaves. After this they set off down the mountain with Bergthor's body. But as soon as they reach level ground this man goes and peers inside his gloves, and they are now full of coins. The farmer and his men turn back at once, wanting to fetch the cauldron, but they cannot find the cave anywhere, and no one has ever found it since. So they had to leave it at that and turn for home, and they carried Bergthor's body down to Haukadal, and the farmer had it buried there on the north side of the church; the place has been called Bergthor's Grave ever since. It is said that the ring from Bergthor's staff is on the church door in Haukadal, and its iron spike is said to have been long used as the church crowbar. And this is the end of the story of Bergthor of Blafell.

J.Á. I 213–14; from Egill Pálsson (d.1881), from oral traditions current in Biskupstúngar. This is one of the comparatively few tales of a friendly giant, well disposed towards his human neighbours and even towards Christianity – the kind of being alluded to in the proverbial saying *tryggr sem tröll*, 'as trusty as a troll'. It has been suggested that these amiable trolls are descended, not from the evil giants of heathen myth, but from the benevolent 'land-spirits', which did sometimes appear as of more than human size (Sveinsson 1940, 143, 147). Even so, the fact that Bergthor is not Christian means that he has to be buried on the *north* side of the church, traditionally reserved for those who do not qualify for proper religious rites. The giants referred to in the opening sentences are characters in the fourteenth-century *Bár>arsaga* chapters 9 and 13, and in the seventeenth-century *Ármannssaga* chapter 10.

Another tale of promised wealth which, when found, seems to be mere leaves, is told of the hoard allegedly hidden in a cave by Flosi, the slayer of Njáll (J.Á. II 92–3). It is of course a familiar international motif that gifts from supernatural beings which seem to be of no value turn into gold – and vice versa.

THE GIANTESS' STAFF

The various supernatural beings which lived inside the rocks and mountains of Iceland were extremely displeased when

Christianity began to spread through the land, and even more so when churches were built. It is said that soon after the church at Thingeyrar was erected, a Night-Troll who lived in the mountain above Vatnsdal got in a huff, and thought herself deeply injured because a church had been built there. This Night-Troll was a giantess. One night she set out, meaning to take her revenge for this annoyance. She went north to the outermost spur of Vatnsdal Mountain, or at any rate to the spot called The Shoulder, and since she had nothing better to hand than her own staff, she took a grip on it and threw it, meaning to smash Thingeyrar Church with it.

As soon as she had flung this staff, she looked round to see how time was getting on, but by then dawn was already breaking in the east. This affected her as it does all Night-Trolls, so that she crashed headlong down over the west side of the mountain, which is a sheer bluff, and came to rest on a ledge, a mere stone's throw from the foot of the bluff, and there she turned into a pillar of stone. And there she still stands to this day, and is known as the Old Woman, up by the farm which takes its name from The Shoulder where she stood when she threw the staff, being called Oxl.

As for the staff, it broke in two as it hurtled through the air, and the first piece did come down pretty close to Thingeyrar Church, for it landed right on the paved path that runs past the south side of the church, where it has been used as a horse-block ever since; it must be nearly three ells long, and there is no more than forty yards between the spot where it lay until 1832 and the church itself. But the other piece of the staff came down to the south of the home-field of Thingeyrar Farm, and this one is a bit shorter; it can be seen built into the corner of the homefield fence, on the right-hand side as one rides up to Thingeyrar.

J.Á. I 216 (*Kerlingin í Vatnsdalsfjalli*), from an old woman in Húnavatnssýsla. He also gives two other legends of trolls flinging rocks at churches (I 216–17), one being very similar to this; the theme, however, is less frequent in Iceland than in Continental Scandinavia, where it forms part of the group ML 5020, 'Trolls Build a Causeway'. Hurling huge boulders at churches is a typical activity of giants and the Devil in local legends throughout Europe; besides their humour, and their usefulness in accounting for some conspicuous rock, these tales carry the implied message that God protects the church against forces seeking to destroy it.

GRYLA

Stories about the ogress called Gryla and her husband Leppa-Ludi can be traced back to medieval times, particularly in her case, and there are many rhymes and jingles about them, especially about Gryla. They were both thought of as trolls, and indeed 'Gryla' appears in a list of she-trolls' names in Snorri's *Edda*; they were man-eaters, like other trolls, attacking children in particular, but also full-grown men. But once people began to give up deliberately terrifying growing children, the belief in Gryla was largely abandoned, since the threat of Gryla had been much used to frighten children out of naughtiness and silly actions, which is why the word *grýla* was used in the thirteenth century for a she-troll or a terrifying bogy, and the word *grýlur* for threats.

Early in her history, Gryla was already represented as a monster, for a passage in *Sturlunga saga* mentions that she has fifteen tails; the same thing is mentioned in a rhyme about her:

> *Gryla rode into the yard;*
> *Fifteen tails had she,*
> *And on each tail a hundred bags,*
> *And twenty children in each bag.*

Again, another rhyme goes:

> *Gryla rode into the yard;*
> *Hoofs she had to walk upon,*

From her brow the long tufts hung;
A bag she bore against her thigh —
The children are in there, thought I.

The longer poems about Gryla do not show her as a beauty either, when they say she has three hundred heads, and three eyes in each head that she spies out children with, and then she and Leppa-Ludi stick them in a big grey bag; or again, where it says that she has deformed nails on every finger, eyes as black as Hell in the back of her neck, goat's horns, and ears which hang down on her shoulders behind and brush against her nose in front. She also had a beard, but it never grew any thicker than tangled yarn, with tufts of matted hair hanging from it; her teeth were like burnt and blackened stones.

As has been mentioned already, Gryla's husband was called Leppa-Ludi; he was very like her, but perhaps not quite so hideous. One rhyme gives the names of twenty children of theirs, and they also had thirteen sons known as the 'Christmas Lads', unless, as some say, these were Gryla's sons by some unknown man before she married Leppa-Ludi. The reason that there are thirteen of them is that the first comes thirteen days before Christmas, and then one more each day, and the last on Christmas Eve. On Christmas Day the first leaves, and so on, one by one, and the last on the last day of Christmas. These Christmas Lads were used for frightening children, like their parents, especially at Christmas time; they come down from the mountains to human dwellings to do various jobs for which each was trained and which most of their names indicate, but they were all only too willing to carry off any children who cried too much or were in any way unruly.

Then, Leppa-Ludi had a bastard son called Skroggur, who was no great improvement on his father; his wife was an elf's daughter, and was named Skjoda. There are long rhymes telling of the exploits of all these persons.

J.Á. I 218–21 (shortened); the description of Grýla in the third paragraph is based on a poem by the Revd Gu>mundur Erlendsson (d. 1670). The various flulur, i.e. long jingling verses, which deal with Grýla and her family can be found in Jón Árnason and Ólafur Daví>sson, *Íslenzkar Gátur* etc., 1887–1903. Similar bugbears and hobgoblins were known in many parts of Europe, associated with St Nicholas' Day, Christmas, or some other festival, and used in the same way to frighten children into good behaviour. Nowadays they play only a minor role compared with the seasonal gift-bringer (St Nicholas, La Befana, etc.); similarly, in modern Iceland Grýla and her sons are only figures of fun, and may even bring presents for children.

A related verse is recorded in a thirteenth-century saga as a threat uttered by a certain Loftr Pálsson in 1221, as he rode onto the farm of an enemy:

> *Here comes Grýla down into the field,*
> *And she has fifteen tails on her.*

This is very close to a rhyme recorded several times in the Faroes in the nineteenth and twentieth centuries:

> *Down comes Grýla from the outer fields,*
> *With forty tails,*
> *A bag on her back, a knife in her hand,*
> *Coming to cut out the stomachs of children*
> *Who cry for meat in Lent.*

This rhyme was associated with a seasonal house-to-house visiting custom in the days preceding Lent, especially in the evening of Shrove Tuesday, called *Grýlukvøld*. The Grýla, described as a monster 'with a sheep's body, but walking upright like a man', would be impersonated by a man wearing a mask and some grotesque costume made from skins, rags, or seaweed; he went from house to house, and would be given gifts of food or drink. The Faroese rhyme and custom persisted from the eighteenth century to the mid-twentieth; it may be that in Iceland too Grýla was at one time impersonated in seasonal custom, as well as being described in rhyme. See Williamson, 247–8; Gunnell 1995, 160–7.

3

WATER-DWELLERS

THEN THE MERMAN LAUGHED

A merman is a dwarf that lives in the sea. There is an old saying in Iceland which many people use as a proverb: 'Then the merman laughed'. As for how it arose, it is said that a certain farmer drew up in his fishing-net a sea-dwarf who called himself a merman, with a big head and broad hands, but shaped like a seal below the navel. He would not teach any of his magic lore to the farmer, so the latter took him ashore, much against his will.

The farmer's wife, a young and lusty woman, came down to the shore and greeted her husband, kissing and fondling him. The farmer was pleased and praised her, but drove his dog away with a blow when it came up with the wife to greet him. Then, when he saw that, the merman laughed. The farmer asks why he laughed, and the merman says: 'At stupidity.'

As the farmer was making his way home from the sea, he stumbled and tripped over a tussock. He cursed the tussock heartily, asking why it had ever been sent by fate to stand on his land. Then the merman laughed (for he was being carried along, against his will), and said: 'This farmer has no sense.'

The farmer kept the merman in his house for three days. Some travelling merchants came there, with wares to sell. Now the farmer had never been able to get boots with soles as thick and strong as he wanted, but these merchants thought they had boots of the best quality. The farmer could take his pick among a hundred pairs, and still he said they were all too thin and would be in holes in no time. Then the merman laughed and said: 'It's clever men that make the biggest fools.'

The farmer could not get any further words of wisdom out of the merman by fair means or foul, except on condition that he took him out to sea again, right back to the very fishing-bank where he had been caught, and then he would squat on the blade of the farmer's oar and answer all his questions, but not otherwise. So, after three days, the farmer did this. And when the dwarf was on the oar-blade, the farmer asked what gear fisherman ought to use if they wanted good catches.

The merman answered: 'Chewed and trodden iron must be used for the hooks, and the forging must be done where one can hear both river and wave, and the hooks must be tempered in horse piss. Use a fishing-line made from a grey bull's sinews, and cord from raw horse-hide. For bait, use birds' gizzards and flounders, but human flesh on the middle bight, and then if you get no catch you're surely fey. The barb of a fishhook must point outwards.'

Then the farmer asked him what was the stupidity he had laughed at when he praised his wife and struck his dog.

The merman answered: 'Your own stupidity, farmer. Your dog loves you as dearly as his own life, but your wife wishes you were dead, and she is a whore. The tussock you cursed covers a treasure destined for you, and there's money in plenty under it; that was why you had no sense, farmer, and why I laughed. And the black boots will last you all your life, for you haven't many days to live – three days, they'll last you three days!'

And with this he plunged off the oar-blade, and so they parted. But everything the merman said proved to be true.

J.Á. I 132–3, from *Tídsfordrif* (1644) by Jón Gu>mundsson the Learned (1574–1658). Another version, with an associated verse, is given by Jón Árnason (I 133–4, tr. Powell and Magnússon 103–6 and Simpson 1988, 236–7), and there are also four manuscript versions (Sveinsson 1929, 113–4). An early literary treatment is the fourteenth-century *Hálfs saga ok*

Hálfsrekka, chapter 7. Sveinsson gives this tale a classification number of its own, 803*, but its Irish and Norwegian analogues are classified as a sub-type of AT 670 'The Animal Languages' (Christiansen and O'Suillibhean, 1963). In Norway and Ireland the central figure is usually a merman, but in Ireland it may also be a leprechaun (cf. O'Sullivan 1966, 179–33; Chesnutt 1999; Erlendsson 1999, 65–73). The story could also be regarded as a variant of ML 4060 'The Mermaid's Message', in which a mermaid, captured and then released, offers warning or advice, but also sometimes mocks her captor for asking only foolish questions.

Similar mockery appears here (but not in the other Icelandic versions) in the merman's sarcastic advice on fishing: to chew and tread iron instead of welding it is impossible, and a barb that points outward will never hold a fish. Nevertheless, the advice seems related to actual superstitions. The same bait, plus a mouse, is said to have been used by fiorbjǫrn kólki, one of the first settlers in Iceland, later reputed a wizard (J.Á. II 130); and a fishing line was thought useless unless a grey bull or grey stallion had been led over it (J.Á. II 554). Cf. the elaborate fishing charm, containing several of the same lines, in Eiríkur Laxdal's *Ólafs saga* fiórhallasonar, *c.*1788 (Sveinsson 1940, 109; 2003, 84).

For the belief that one among the innumerable tussocks in an Icelandic field may conceal treasure, cf. p.201. The present version implies that the farmer was unable to identify the tussock again, and so lost his chance of wealth, but other variants say that he did find the gold, and so believed the remarks about his wife and dog.

THE SEA-COWS

S ome fishermen from Hofdi once rowed out to the fishing-banks off Latrastrand, and there caught a mermaid on their hook; they brought her home with them to Hofdi. She spoke very seldom; she said her home was in the sea, and that she had been cleaning her mother's kitchen chimney when they caught her. Time and again she would beg them to take her back out to sea and throw her in again at the same fishing-bank where they had caught her, but they would not, as they would rather that she should get used to life on land, for she was beautiful, and had all sorts of skills. She stayed at Hofdi for a year, during which time she embroidered the vestments which have been used ever since in Laufas Church.

When the year was up she was taken out to sea again, for people saw she would never be happy on land. She promised them before-hand that she would send some cows up on land; she said that as soon as the cows came ashore men must be ready to catch hold of them and burst the bladder they had between their nostrils, for otherwise they would at once run back into the sea. Then the girl was allowed to slip back into the water over the fishing-bank where she had been caught.

Not long after, twelve cows came up out of the sea and made straight for Hofdi; they were as grey as the sea itself. The place where they came ashore is now called Kvigudalir, 'Cow Dales'. Six of these cows were caught and tamed – and excellent beasts they proved to be – but the other six escaped.

J.Á. I 134–5 (*Kvígudalir á Látraströnd*), from the Revd Arnljótur Ólafsson (d.1904). Another story tells how a man intercepted a herd of sea-cows being driven down to the water by 'a little lad', but could catch only one calf; in another, a man finds eighteen cows in his byre, and catches nine before the rest plunge into a lake (J.Á. I 135). Bursting the bladder is mentioned in both, and also in Jón Árnason's second version of 'Then the Merman Laughed', where the merman sends seven cows ashore in grati-tude for his release, but the farmer can secure only one. The owners of sea-cows were often supposed to be, not mermen, but the 'Sea People', i.e. underwater elves (cf. the stories of elfin cows disenchanted by drawing blood, pp.37–9 above). The belief in the existence of sea-cows goes back to the sixteenth century, for on a map of Iceland printed in 1595 some are shown at the foot of Eyjafjöll labelled *vaccae marinae* (Sveinsson 1940, 77; 2003, 84). Fairy cattle from underwater are common in Irish, Welsh and Scottish lore; for an Irish tale of a mermaid captured and released, see

'The Child from the Sea', O'Sullivan 1966, 188; Briggs 1971, I 319.

THE WATER HORSE

The Water Horse is named either Nykur or Nennir, and lives in rivers or lakes or even the open sea. He looks just like a horse, usually a grey but sometimes a black one, but all his hoofs are turned back to front and the tufts on his pasterns point backwards. However, he is in no way limited to this form; it is characteristic of him to change suddenly into various shapes, just as he chooses. In winter when cracks appear in the ice and cause loud booming noises, men say that the Nykur is neighing. He begets foals like other stallions do, but always in the water, though it has sometimes happened that he has got an ordinary mare with foal. It is characteristic of all horses descended from a Nykur that they lie down whenever they are ridden or led through water that reaches to their bellies, and this is a trait they inherit from the Nykur. A Nykur will often appear on land near rivers or lakes that are difficult to cross; he seems quiet enough at such times, and tempts people to ride across on him, but as soon as they are up on his back he rushes wildly into the water, lies down flat in it, and drags his rider down too. The Nykur cannot bear to hear his own name, or any word that sounds at all like it, and if he does he shies violently and gallops into the water.

All over Iceland people believed in the Nykur, so in almost every district there are stories of one living in this or that river or lake, especially those with strong currents. In the island of Grimsey, off the north coast, people believed that a Nykur lived in the sea and neighed whenever he knew that the islanders had gone to fetch a cow from the mainland; the cows went mad at his neighing, flung themselves in the sea, and so were drowned. Not before the middle of the nineteenth century did the men of Grimsey dare keep a cow on their island.

J.Á. I 135–6. The belief in the water horse is old in Iceland; it is already mentioned in *Landnamabók* chapters 56–7. The name *nykur* is cognate with the general Scandinavian word for a water-spirit, whether in animal or human shape. Unlike the Scottish kelpie, the *nykur* does not take on human shape (except in the ballad *Elenarljó*>, where he appears as a young man to woo the heroine, with the intention of drowning her). He can, however, appear as a cow with backward-turning hooves; unlike the excellent sea-cows, this beast is savage and unmilkable.

There is also a vaguer type of water-monster, the *skrímsli*, variously described as like a whale, like two horses joined at the rump, or as half human and half animal (J.Á. I 138–41, tr. Powell and Magnússon 108–10). Rivers and lakes may also be said to be infested by monstrous skates, or by water-serpents, for which see below, pp. 116–17.

THE WATER HORSE HEARS HIS NAME

Once, a shepherd girl was searching for her sheep; she had walked a long way and was very tired. Then she sees a grey horse, and is very pleased; she puts her garter on him as a bridle, lays her apron across his back, leads him to a tussock, and prepares to mount him. But just as she is about to mount, she says: 'I don't think I fancy getting on his back! Aren't I a ninny!' Then the horse shied violently, dashed into a lake nearby, and vanished. Then the girl saw what kind of a creature it had been – it was a Water Horse. It is characteristic of a Water Horse that he must never hear his own name, or he returns into the water where he lives; he has two names, Nykur and Nennir, and so he went off as soon as the girl said 'ninny'. The same thing happens if a Nykur hears the word 'Devil' spoken.

Once, three or four children were playing. Not far from their farm was a broad lake with smooth gravel banks, and the children were on the banks by the water. There they saw a grey horse, and went to have a look at it. Then one of the children climbs onto its back, and the others too, one after the other, till only the eldest was left. They urged him to come too, saying this old pack-horse had plenty room enough on his long back, even if they all got on at once. But the child refused to get on, and the others called him a ninny. Then the horse shied, and hurtled out into the lake with all the other children on his back. The one who had stayed behind went home and told the tale, and people knew that this must have been the Nykur; he was never seen again, nor the children either.

J.Á. I 137–8 (*Nennir*), from widespread tales attached to many lakes. In order to convey the pun, I have added the word 'ninny' to the crucial remarks; the original turns on the verb *nenna* 'to feel like doing something' – *eg nenni ekki á bak*, 'I don't feel like getting on its back'. The heroine of the *Elenarljó>* is saved by the lucky use of the same word. A Faroese version neatly achieves its effect by having one little child call out to his brother Nicholas, 'Nika! Nika!' (Kvideland and Sehmsdorf, 257).

A Scottish kelpie too will occasionally flee at the threat that its name will be uttered aloud, though whether this means a secret personal name or the generic term 'kelpie' is not clear (cf. the story of the kelpie of Orbost, Swire 1961, 146).

The numerous Danish and Swedish parallels to the second part of this story turn on the water horse's fear of the name of God; he rushes off when the last child exclaims: 'By the Lord Jesus' Cross! I've never seen a longer horse!' (Lindow, 120–1; Simpson 1988, 234) The *nykur* too sometimes dreads the name of God (Jón fiorkelsson, fijó>sögur og munnmæli, 1899, 445).

THE WATER HORSE MADE TO WORK

It happened once that the farmers of the parish of Bard (or some say Holt) in the district of Fljot had to build a wall round their churchyard. Early one morning they had all gathered for the work except one old man; this man was thought to be pretty spiteful, and was generally disliked. Time wore on towards midday, and he still had not come, and the rest thought he was taking a long time over it. Just on the stroke of noon they saw him coming, leading a grey horse behind him. As soon as he arrives he is met by angry words from those who had got there early, for coming late for his share of the work. The old fellow keeps his temper, and asks what work he is to do. He was sent to join the group whose job it was to carry turf and other building materials for the wall, and he says he likes this job well enough.

His grey horse was very rough and vicious towards the other horses carrying turf; he tore himself free from the horse in front, and he bit them and kicked them until none of the rest would stand up to him. The men thought this a great nuisance, and agreed to lay heavier loads on him, but it was no use – even with loads twice as heavy he moved just as briskly and never stopped his tricks until he had driven all the other horses away, and then there was only him left. Then the old man takes this pack-horse of his and piles as large a load onto his back as had been loaded onto all the other horses put together for a single trip, and led him off, and then he was quiet enough. In this way, using the grey horse, the man shifted all the building materials down to the churchyard.

But when it was all finished, he takes the bridle off the horse close beside the churchyard wall, just where it was freshly built, and lashes the horse across the loins with the bridle as he lets him go. The grey horse does not like this; he ups with his hind quarters and drives both heels against the church wall which they had been building all day, and knocks a great hole in it – and no wall has ever stood firm on that spot, however often it was rebuilt, till in the end people came to use this as the gateway for the church. And the last thing anybody saw of that packhorse was that he galloped off as soon as he was free, and never stopped till he plunged into

Holt Lake; and then they all felt certain that this must have been the Nykur.

J.Á. I 136–7, from Sigur>ur Gu>mundsson (d.1874). The same story was told of the master-magician Hálfdan of Fell by Ólafur the Old in the late seventeenth century (J.Á. I xix). Similar tales are found in Scotland, the Faroes, and many parts of Scandinavia, the horse usually being used for ploughing or other farm work (Lindow, 119–20; Kvideland and Sehmsdorf, 258–9); among the means mentioned for mastering the horse are a magic bridle, a cow's halter, and the Sign of the Cross. The motif of the ruined wall is common also in troll stories (see above, p.81).

The legend is also common in Ireland, where it has been given the number 4086. For a discussion of this and other Irish water-horse legends, and their possible links with Scotland and Scandinavia, see Bo Almquist, 'Waterhorse Legends' in *Béaloideas* 59 (1991), 107–20.

THE SEAL'S SKIN

There was once some man from Myrdal in Eastern Iceland who went walking among the rocks by the sea one morning before anyone else was up. He came to the mouth of a cave, and inside the cave he could hear merriment and dancing, but outside it he saw a great many sealskins. He took one skin away with him, carried it home, and locked it away in a chest. Later in the day he went back to the mouth of the cave; there was a young and lovely woman sitting there, and she was stark naked, and weeping bitterly. This was the seal whose skin it was that the man had taken. He gave the girl some clothes, comforted her, and took her home with him. She grew very fond of him, but did not get on so well with other people. Often she would sit alone and stare out to sea.

After some while the man married her, and they got on well together, and had several children. As for the skin, the man always kept it locked up in the chest, and kept the key on him wherever he went. But after many years, he went fishing one day and forgot it under his pillow at home. Other people say that he went to church one Christmas with the rest of his household, but that his wife was ill and stayed at home; he had forgotten to take the key out of the pocket of his everyday clothes when he changed. Be that as it may, when he came home again the chest was open, and both wife and skin were gone. She had taken the key and examined the chest, and there she had found the skin; she had been unable to resist the temptation, but had said farewell to her children, put the skin on, and flung herself into the sea.

Before the woman flung herself into the sea, it is said that she spoke these words:

> *Woe is me! Ah, woe is me!*
> *I have seven bairns on land,*
> *And seven in the sea.*

It is said that the man was broken-hearted about this. Whenever he rowed out fishing afterwards, a seal would often swim round and round his boat, and it looked as if tears were running from its eyes. From that time on, he had excellent luck in his fishing, and various valuable things were washed ashore on his beach. People often noticed, too, that when the children he had had by this woman went walking along the seashore, a seal would show itself near the edge of the water and keep level with them as they walked along the shore, and would toss them jellyfish and pretty shells. But never did their mother come back to land again.

J.Á. I 632–3, from the Revd Skúli Gíslason (d.1888). A fine example of ML 4080, 'The Seal Woman', also classifiable as a sub-type of AT 400, 'The Man on a Quest for his Lost Wife'. Six other versions are known from Iceland, the earliest being from a work by Jón Gu>mimdsson the Learned, 1641 (J.Á. I xiii, Maurer 173, and four in manuscript); see Simpson 1988, 241–2, for a translation of J.Á.'s second version. Seals were said to be descended from Pharaoh's soldiers, drowned in the Red Sea, and to lay aside their skins and resume human form once a year, on Midsummer Eve, or on the twelfth day of Christmas; the term 'Sea People' was sometimes applied to them. Similar tales are common in Scotland, Ireland, the Orkneys and Faroes, and in Norway; for the Scottish and Irish tales and beliefs, see Thomson, 1965. For a Faroese version, see Kvideland and Sehmsdorf, 265–6.

The Water-Snake of Lagarfljot

It happened once, long ago, that there was a woman living on a farm in the district near Lake Lagarfljot. She had a grown-up daughter, and she gave this daughter a gold ring.

Then the girl says; 'How can I make the most of this gold, mother?'

'Lay it under a Heath Snake,' says the woman.

So then the girl catches a Heath Snake, puts the gold underneath it, and lays it in her trinket box. There the serpent lies for some days. But when the girl goes to take a look inside the box, the snake has grown so big that the panels of the box have begun to split open. Then the girl grows frightened, snatches up the box, and hurls it out into the lake, with everything that's in it.

Now a long time passes by, and then people begin to become aware of the serpent in the lake. He began to attack men and animals that were crossing the lake; sometimes, too, he would crawl up onto the banks and snort out poison, most horribly. All this was beginning to cause a great deal of trouble, but nobody knew of any way to cure it.

Then two Lapps were sent for; they were to kill the snake, and take the gold. They dived down into the lake, but they soon came up again. These Lapps said they had met their match, and more, down there, and that it would not be easy to kill the snake or to take the gold. They said there was a second snake under the gold, and this one was far more evil than the first. So then they had tied the snake down with two fetters; one they had placed just behind the fins, the other near the tail.

Therefore the snake cannot harm anyone now, man or beast, but sometimes it happens that he thrusts a hump of his back up above the surface, and whenever that is seen it is always thought a sign of dire events to come, for instance bad seasons, or a great shortage of grass. Those who do not believe in this serpent say that it is only a trail of floating foam, and they repeat stories about how some priest, not long ago, rowed right across the spot where it looked as if the serpent was, so as to prove his statement that there was nothing there at all.

J.Á. I 638–9, from a schoolboy in Múlasýsla in 1845. This monster is first mentioned in the Icelandic Annals for 1345 (*Skálholts Annáll*), and many more sightings have since been alleged; for accounts of repeated sightings in 1749–50 and again in 1819, see J.Á. I 640–1. The creature is sometimes described as like a huge snake with humps and / or spikes on it, sometimes as like a monstrous horse. There are several other rivers and lakes which have water-snakes in them and there too it is said that a small 'worm' was thrown into the water, together with gold to which it clung, and that both the beast and the treasure grew large in the depths (Erlingsson, 62).

The 'Heath Snake' mentioned here, the *lýngorm*, was a mythical creature which, like the dragon, had a particular affinity for gold; a piece of gold laid under it would multiply, and the serpent would grow at the same rate, so that it soon would become a menacing monster. The motif makes its first appearance in Iceland in the fourteenth century, in *Ragnars saga lo>brókar*, where it serves as introduction to a 'Dragon Slayer' tale. In later Icelandic lore such serpents are often identified with lake-haunting monsters, as here; there is also said to be one in the depths of the cave Surtshellir. There is a strong general similarity between these legends and those of the dragon-like *lindorm* elsewhere in Scandinavia, the monster-snakes of Scottish lochs, and the horse-headed water-serpents in Irish lakes and rivers; the Scottish and Irish monsters, however, are not usually associated with sunken treasures.

Lapps, *Finnar*, have been regarded as particularly powerful magicians ever since medieval times; they are mentioned as such in many sagas. In ML 3060, 'Banning the Snakes', common in Norway, a Finn is hired to rid a district of snakes but in so doing is himself killed by a *lindorm* (cf. Christiansen 1964, 41–2).

4

GHOSTS

'Mother Mine, Don't Weep, Weep'

There was once a girl who was a servant on a farm. She had become pregnant, had given birth to her child, and had put it in the open to die, as was not uncommon in Iceland, even though harsh penalties of outlawry or death were imposed for such crimes. Some time after, it so happened that there was to be one of those parties with dancing and mumming which were once so common in Iceland and were called *vikivaki* dances, and this same girl was invited to the *vikivaki*. But she did not possess any showy and expensive dresses good enough for such a merry gathering as a *vikivaki* used to be in the old days, and as she was a girl who was fond of finery, she was very upset to think that she would have to stay at home and miss the dancing.

One day, at the time when the dance was being held, this servant girl was busy with some other women milking ewes in the sheep-fold, and began telling another milkmaid how she had no clothes to go to the *vikivaki* in. As soon as she has finished speaking, they both hear this verse, spoken by a voice from under the wall of the sheep-fold:

> *Mother mine, don't weep, weep,*
> *As you milk the sheep, sheep;*
> *I can lend my rags to you,*
> *So you'll go a-dancing too,*
> *You'll go a-dancing too.*

The girl who had put her child out to die thought she had had a message from it, and this verse impressed her so deeply that for the rest of her life she was never in her right mind.

J.Á. I 225 (*'Mó>ir mín í kví, kví'*); a tale current throughout Iceland. Babies exposed at birth and secretly buried in unhallowed ground are known as *útbur>ir* (a term used in medieval times for any child which, dying unbaptised, had to be buried outside the churchyard). They are said to make particularly vicious ghosts, wailing and screaming near their place of burial, or crawling about on one knee and elbow, with their feet and hands crossed; they wear only the ragged cloth their mothers wrapped them in to bury them. They try to lead men astray in fog or in the dark, and if they can make three circles round anyone, he will go mad (J.Á. I 224–5).

Similar beliefs are common throughout Scandinavia; cf. ML 4025 'Infants Killed Before Baptism Haunt Mother'. See Simpson (1988) 99–101; Kvideland and Sehmsdorf, 113–18; Juha Pentikäinen, *The Nordic Dead-Child Tradition* (Helsinki, 1968); Bo Almquist, 'Norwegian Dead-Child Traditions Westward Bound', in *Viking Ale*, ed. Éilís Ní Dhuibhne-Almquist and Seámas Ó Catháin (Aberystwyth, 1991), 155-67.

Repeated words or lines in a verse, as here, are a sign that it is spoken by a ghost or other supernatural being (cf. pp. 125, 212); the effect is felt as sinister.

A *vikivaki* was a prolonged party held at major festivals such as Christmas and New Year; besides feasting, there were songs and dances – particularly a type of individual dance for one man and one woman, each singing alternate verses, often amorous or bawdy. This dance was also itself called *vikivaki*; texts of the songs are in Árnason and Daví>sson 1887–1903, III. The entertainment also included mumming dancers, with hobby-horses, men-women, or mummers dressed as rams or stags (Dag Strömbäck, 'Cult Remnants in Icelandic Dramatic Dances', *Arv* IV, 1948, 132–5). The oldest full account of a *vikivaki* party is of the early seventeenth century, but Bishop Jón Ogmundarson (d. 1121) already denounced a type of singing dance exactly like the *vikivaki* dance.

'ISN'T IT FUN IN THE DARK!'

In the old days, and right into the nineteenth century, it was customary for someone to keep watch beside a corpse, and this was generally done with a light burning, unless the night was very bright. Once, a certain magician died; his mind had been full of the old heathen ways, and he had been an unpleasant person to deal with, so there were not many people willing to come and keep watch by his body. However, one man was found to do the job; he was a very strong man, with a fearless heart. His vigil went well.

On the last night before the body was to be put in its coffin, the light went out a little before dawn broke. Then the body sat up and said: 'Isn't it fun in the dark!'

The watcher replied: 'You won't gain much out of it!' and then recited this verse:

> *All the earth is shining now,*
> *Night has fled away;*
> *The candle's out, but dust art thou –*
> *Be silent for today!*

Then he flung himself on the corpse and forced it down on its back, and it stayed quiet for the rest of the night.

J.Á. I 226–7, from the Revd Skúli Gíslason (d.1888). Stories of the dead speaking or moving before burial must have been common at all periods; there are instances in *Eyrbyggja saga* chapter 51 and *The Saga of Eirik the Red* chapter 4. Mastering a ghost by wrestling is the commonest Icelandic method, both in sagas and folktales.

A similar tale (J.Á. I 226, 601; translated in Kvideland and Sehmsdorf, 103) tells of a woman sewing a sorcerer's corpse into its shroud. When she had almost finished, he spoke: 'You still have to bite the thread from the needle.' 'I mean to break, not bite it, curse you!' said she, snapped the needle in two, and stuck the bits into his feet (to stop him walking, cf. p.155). Thus she avoided the fate of her predecessors, who, less resource-ful, had been killed or driven mad.

THE LOVERS

Once a lad and a girl lived on the same farm; they were engaged, and loved each other very much. He had to go to sea that year, but before he left they talked together and he prom-ised the girl that he would write to her regularly and at length. Then he went, and so time passed till Christmas. Around Christmas time, the girl began to dream frequently of her lover, and the dreaming grew so insistent that she could hardly get a few hours' quiet rest. He would start telling her all sorts of things, about himself and about other people too.

On that farm there was an old woman who was rather wise about such matters; the girl went to her and told her about her dreams, and that she could not sleep in peace.

The old woman did not seem much perturbed, but said to the girl: 'This evening you shall sleep, but I will see to the door of the building you sleep in.'

That evening the girl went to sleep; she dreamed that her lover came to the window and said: 'It was wrong of you to lock the door against me. As things are, I will never be able to come to you again; but had they been otherwise, I would have wanted to be your Dream Guide.'

Then he recited this verse:

> Our bodies sleep beneath the sea,
> Where no harm comes nigh us;

Yet in Heaven's peace are we,
Praising God the Highest.

Then he went away, but the girl woke up, and she was so crazed that she ran out, meaning to kill herself, but there were people there who had not yet gone to bed, and they managed to catch her. She recovered completely, and the dead man never visited her again.

J.Á. I 231; a tale from Skar>sströnd in Western Iceland. There are several such stories (J.Á. I 228–32) of ghosts appearing in dreams to tell where their bodies, lost at sea or in the wild uplands, might be found: they often speak a verse, but without any sinister repetition, for their purpose is harmless. In the present instance, the verse addresses an issue important to a seafaring community: whether those lost at sea can attain salvation in the same way as those laid in the consecrated ground of a churchyard. A 'Dream Man' is a ghost regularly visiting the dreams of someone gifted with second sight to act as his guide and informant; see for example, the traditions about Jón Danielsson (d.1855), who was reputed to have two such guides (J.Á. I 426–7).

MURDER WILL OUT

O nce a grave was being dug in some churchyard, and in the course of the digging a skull came to light, and there was a knitting needle driven right through it. The priest kept the skull till Mass on the next Holy Day. He waited till everyone was inside the church, and then hung the skull up over the church door. After the service, the priest went out first with his altar-servers, and watched the people as they came out. They noticed nothing, so they went to check whether anyone had stayed inside, and there was one very old woman cowering up against the back wall, and they had to use force before she would go out. Then three drops of blood dripped from the skull onto the old woman's kerchief, and she said: 'Murder will out at last.'

Then she confessed that she had killed her first husband by driving a knitting needle into his head; she had been young at the time, and had been married to him against her will, and they had not lived together long. The woman had prepared his body for burial herself, and no one else had thought anything about it. Later she had married someone else, but he too was dead by now. It is said that this old woman was executed by drowning, as women were if they had killed their children.

J.Á. I 232–3 (*'Upp koma svik um si>ir'*), from the Revd Skúli Gíslason; a story current in Vatnsdalur. The theme of murder revealed is rare in Iceland, probably because open slaying is so much more common than secret murder in her history, sagas, and traditions.

JON FLAK

There was a man called Jon and nicknamed Jon Flak. He was an odd sort of man, and was not much liked by his neighbours; he was inclined to provoke people over petty matters, and very few managed to get their own back on him. When Jon died, the gravediggers played a trick on him by making the grave lie north and south. Jon was buried at the back of the choir in Muli church-yard, but every night afterwards he haunted the gravediggers, and repeated this verse:

> *Cold the earth at choir-back;*
> *All alone there lies Jon Flak.*
> *All the rest lie east and west,*
> *Everyone but Jon Flak,*
> *Everyone but Jon Flak.*

Others say that the verse was heard coming out of Jon's grave. Be that as it may, he never stopped this nagging until he was dug up again and laid east and west like other men.

J.Á. I 233, from an old woman of Borgarfjör>ur, and a schoolboy from Northern Iceland in 1845. This tale was already known to Jón Ólafsson of Grunnavík (1705–79). Its numerous variants differ in the reason they give for Jón Flak's unorthodox burial; some say he was suspected of suicide, others that his spiteful wife arranged it so as to pay off old scores, others that the burial was too hasty because of stormy weather. The hero's nickname is sometimes Hrak; the verse varies only slightly. J.Á. I 234–41 contains eleven other stories of ghosts complaining of or revenging themselves for disrespectful treatment; some are included here; for others, see Powell and Magnússon 159–60, Craigie 289–90.

BURNING THE COFFINS

In the north of Iceland there was a priest named Ketill Jonsson, who lived at Husavik in the 1530s. He once ordered some coffins to be dug up from his churchyard, and said he was doing so because there was so little space left, and that these coffins took up space but served no useful purpose, since the bodies were quite rotted away.

One day it so happened that three old women were at work in his kitchen, busy burning these coffins, when a spark jumped from the fire and landed on one of them; it quickly set her clothes on fire, and those of the other two also, for they were all very close to one another. The fire was so fierce that they were all dead before anyone could come to put it out.

That night the priest dreamed that a man came to him and said: 'You'll never succeed in making clear space in the churchyard, however much you dig our coffins up. I've just killed your three old women for you, in revenge for what you did to us, and they'll take up some room in the churchyard. And I'll kill plenty more, if you don't stop these ways of yours.'

And so the man went off; but the priest woke up, and he never dug up coffins from the churchyard again.

J.Á. I 237 (*Ketill prestur í Húsavík*), from a story current in Skar>sströnd. Ketill Jónsson was priest at Húsavík *c.*1537.

'GIVE ME MY BONE, GUNNA!'

One winter, a servant girl named Gudrun, who was a dairy-maid on a farm that had a church attached to it, had lost or broken the small, shallow, open oil-lamp generally used in the cow-house; she hit on the idea of taking a broken bit of a human skull that had been dug up in the churchyard and using this instead of the cow-house lamp, with oil burning in it.

In spite of this, nothing happened until Christmas was past and gone. But on New Year's Eve, just as this girl was about to carry a light out to the cow-house, and was, as usual, using the broken skull as a lamp, a voice called to her through the window and said: 'Give me my bone, Gunna!'

Gudrun was not at all dismayed; she picked up the skull just as it was, with the light burning in it, flung it on the floor, trod on it, and said: 'Come and get it then, curse you!'

Other people say Gudrun simply flung the bit of skull in the direction from which she heard the voice coming, but did not tread on it. But whichever way it was, no harm came to the girl.

J.Á. I 237–8, from Sigur>ur Gu>mundsson (d.1874). This tale and the next are variants of AT 366 'The Man from the Gallows'. It has English parallels; some are serious, such as the tale of the old woman who picked up a set of teeth in Perranzabuloe churchyard (R. Hunt, *Popular Romances of the*

West of England, 1865, 452–3); others are nursery tales told as gruesome jokes ('The Bone', 'Teeny-Tiny', Briggs 1970 II 512, 561–2).

'Gunna' is a common diminutive of 'Gudrun', but the ghost probably uses it to avoid pronouncing *Gu>* 'God' (cf. below, pp.146–50, 'The Deacon of Myrka').

'My Jawbones!'

There was once a parish priest who was in the habit of ordering that all old buried bones unearthed in his churchyard should be brought into his house and burnt. It happened one day, as it often did, that when a corpse was being buried in his churchyard some old bones were unearthed, and these were gathered by the cook, on the priest's orders. But because the bones had got wet when they were dug up, either through rain or snow, the cook could not burn them straight away, and had to lay them near the fire and even on the hearthstone to dry them.

While they were drying, the cook heard, as she was busy cooking in the twilight, a faint voice from somewhere near the hearth, saying: 'My jawbones, my jawbones!'

She heard the same words repeated a second time. So then she began to look about among the human bones which lay all round the hearth near her, to see what the cause of this could be; but she found no human jawbones there.

Then she hears the voice for the third time, saying even more piteously than before: 'Oh, my jawbones, my jawbones!'

So then she sets to and searches still more thoroughly, and finds the two jawbones of a child, linked together; they had fallen from their place on the hearthstone into a corner of the hearth, and were almost beginning to burn. Now she understands that the spirit of the child whose bones these were must be unwilling that they should be burned, so she takes and wraps them in a linen cloth, and puts them into the next grave that was dug in the churchyard. After that, there were no more strange happenings.

J.Á. I 238–9, from Markús Gíslason, a schoolboy, in Mýrasýsla. A more distant variant of AT 366.

THE DEAD MAN'S NIGHTCAP

On a farm beside a church there lived, among others, a young boy and a girl. The boy made a habit of scaring the girl, but she had got so used to it that she was never frightened of anything, for if she did see something she thought it was the boy trying to scare her.

One day it so happened that the washing had been done, and that among the things there were many white nightcaps, such as were in fashion then. In the evening the girl was told to fetch in the washing, which was out in the churchyard. She runs out, and begins to pick up the washing. When she has almost finished, she sees a white spectre sitting on one of the graves. She thinks to herself that the lad is planning to scare her, so she runs up and snatches the spectre's cap off (for she thought the boy had taken one of the nightcaps) and says: 'Now don't you start trying to scare me this time!'

So she went indoors with the washing; the boy had been indoors the whole time. They started sorting out the washing; there was one nightcap too many now, and it was earthy on the inside. Then the girl was scared.

Next morning the spectre was still sitting on the grave, and people did not know what to do about it, as nobody dared take the cap back, and so they sent word all round the district, asking for advice. There was one old man in the district who declared that it would be impossible to stop something bad coming of it, unless the girl herself took the cap back to the spectre and placed it on its head in silence, and that there ought to be many people there to watch.

The girl was forced to go with the cap and place it on the spectre's head, and so she went, though her heart was not much in it, and she placed the cap on the head of the spectre, and when she had done so she said: 'Are you satisfied now?'

But at this the dead man started to his feet, struck her, and said; 'Yes! And you, are you satisfied?'

And with these words he plunged down into his grave. The girl fell down at the blow, and when men ran to pick her up, she was already dead. The boy was punished because he used to scare her, for it was considered that the whole unfortunate affair had been his fault, and he gave up scaring people. And that is the end of this tale.

J.Á. I 239, from Jón Bjarnarson of Brei>uvík. This fine tale does not fit any of the Types in the AT index, for in the humorous AT 1676 group no real ghost is involved. A very close parallel has been recorded in Ulster, in which a bold girl snatches a sheet from a figure in a graveyard, knowing that a lad has planned to scare her, but it is a ghost's shroud; a priest forces her to take the sheet back; she is unharmed, because she is carrying a baby as protection, but never again risks passing a graveyard alone (Linda May Ballard, 'Before Death and Beyond', in *The Folklore of Ghosts,* ed. H.R. E. Davidson and W.M.S. Russell, 1981, 34–6). There are also English tales in which a trickster is justly punished by the arrival of a real devil or ghost, but in these the intended victim of the hoax is unharmed (Briggs 1971, I 23–4, 38, 541, 594–5). The girl in the present story would presumably have been safe if she had not been rude to the ghost and broken the rule of silence.

THE BRIDEGROOM AND THE DEAD MAN

Once, there were four men digging a grave for some corpse or other; some people say it was in the churchyard at Reykholar. They were all cheerful fellows, and one of them, a lively young man, was the greatest joker of the lot. When the grave began to be fairly deep, many bones came up in the digging, and among them there was one most remarkably big thigh-bone from a man's leg. The digger who was so fond of a joke picked up this bone, weighed it in his hand, and measured it against himself, and they do say that when this thigh-bone had one end resting on level ground the other end came up to his hip – and yet he was a full-grown man, of average height.

Now as he was doing this, this young man says, as a joke: 'Unless I'm much mistaken, this fellow must have been a good wrestler; it would be fun to have him at one's wedding feast in due course.'

The others took up the idea, but they talked rather less about it than he did. After which, the man puts the thigh-bone aside with the other bones that had been dug up.

There is nothing more to tell of until five years later, when this same young man is about to get married, and the banns have been read out twice. Then the girl he is engaged to has a dream, three nights running, in which she thinks she sees a terrifyingly big man come to her in her sleep and ask her whether her fiancé remembers now how he jeered at him once, a few years ago; and on the third night he adds that they won't be able to avoid having him as a guest at the wedding. The girl took no notice, but she began to feel oppressed in her sleep, especially as the man was so very big.

She had said nothing to her fiancé about this dream until she had dreamt of the same man three times, but then, next morning, she says to her sweetheart: 'Who are you meaning to ask to our wedding, dear heart?'

'I don't know yet, my dear,' says he. 'I haven't started thinking about it yet; I meant to get the calling of the banns over first.'

'Then you haven't asked anyone already?' says she.

The man says he can't remember doing so, and begins to rack his brains – and he thought it strange that she should be so persistent in questioning him about this. After some thought, he says that the long and the short of it is that he has not actually asked anybody yet, but that, true enough, a few years before he had once said as a joke, about a thigh-bone that had come up out of a grave, that it would be fun to have such a tall man at one's wedding feast in due course; but he could not recall asking anyone else, apart from that.

At this, his fiancée looked rather grave and said that that was not the sort of joke one ought to make, least of all about the bones of the dead – 'and now I had better tell you,' says she, 'that the man you jeered at like that has quite made up his mind to come to our wedding feast.'

Then she told him about all her dreams, and what words the big man had spoken the night before. Her sweetheart was rather alarmed, and says that she had certainly spoken a true word in saying that jokes of that sort were best left unsaid.

Then he goes off to sleep as usual that evening, but during the night he thinks he sees coming towards him a terrifyingly huge man, like a giant, all frowning and scowling, who, he thinks, asks him whether he means to keep his promise, given five years before, and have him as a guest at his wedding. The man was shaking with fear, but he said that so it must be. The other answered that he could not get out of it, like it or not, and that he need never have sneered at his bones, and that he was going to suffer for it now. After that, the ghost goes off, and the man sleeps on till morning, when he tells his fiancée about his dream, and begs her to give him some advice.

She said that he must get hold of some timber and a builder, and have him quickly build an outhouse which would match this man's size, by what they had seen of it in both their dreams, so that he would be able to stand upright in it; and the inside must be as long and as broad as its height to the level of the cross-beam. Also, he must have this outhouse decked out with hangings, just as it is the custom to deck a bridal hall, and there he must lay a table for this guest on his own, with a white tablecloth on it, and set before him some churchyard mould in a dish and some water in a flask (for he would take no other food), and set a chair by the table, and have a bed in the outhouse too in case the man wished to rest, and he must have three candles on the table beside him. The bridegroom must escort him to this place, but must take great care not to walk ahead of him, nor to stand under the same roof with him. Nor should he agree to any request or offer of his, whatever he might suggest, and he should talk to him as little as possible, but lock the shed and leave him as soon as he had offered him what was set on the table. So now the bridegroom has everything done as the bride had stipulated – an outhouse built, standing on its own and of a suitable size, and everything set out in it, just as has been said.

Now time wears on to the day of the wedding feast, and the marriage service is held in the usual way. Next, everybody sat down for the feasting, and in the same way they all got up from the table later on, when it had got quite dark, and still nothing had happened. After this, people were moving about the room, some drinking, some chatting, but the bridal pair were sitting quietly, as is the custom. Then there comes a mighty knock at the door, and nobody is in a hurry to open it; the bride nudges the groom, but he turns quite pale. A little time goes by, and then there comes another single knock, a far heavier one. Then the bride takes the groom by the hand and leads him to the door, much against his will, and opens it. They both see a monstrously tall man standing there, and he says he has come to sit at their wedding feast. So the bride pushes the groom out to go and welcome his guest, praying that God give him strength, and she herself goes back in.

As for the groom, he goes off with this man to the outbuilding he had had built for him, and ushers him into it. The stranger wants him to walk in ahead of him, but this he will not do. So in the end the other goes in first, and as he does, he says: 'Another time you'll take good care not to sneer at dead men's bones.'

The bridegroom pretends not to have heard, and says that he hopes the other will enjoy what has been laid ready for him, and not be angry with him for not being able to stay with him. The stranger urges the bridegroom to come in there with him all the same, even if only for a moment, but he will not do so, not on any account.

Then the dead man says: 'Even if you can't stay beside me this time, nor even come inside the same building as me, I suppose you will do one thing for me – come and visit me in return.'

But this the bridegroom flatly refused, and so slams the door and locks it. Then he goes back to the bridal party, where everything was pretty quiet, for everyone had been reduced to silence by what had happened. Only the bride still behaved cheerfully. After this, the guests took themselves off little by little, and the young couple settled down for the night, and they slept till morning.

Next morning the young husband wanted to go and see what had become of his latest guest of the evening before, but the bride says he must not take so much as a single step in that direction unless she comes with him. So they both of them go out to the outhouse, she going ahead to open the door; the guest has quite gone, and he has finished the water in the flask, but has scattered the earth from the dish all over the floor.

'I thought as much,' said the woman. 'If you had gone to this building without me, and if you had put one foot in this earth, you would have passed into the ghost's power, and would never have returned to the world of men. But it won't hurt me even if I do step in it, and so I'll sweep and scrub the building.'

But other people say that as the ghost was just leaving he went to the door of the room where the feasters were, or to that of the room where the young couple were feasting, and spoke this verse:

> *There's no thanks from your guest,*
> *For nothing did I taste*

> *But water plain and cold*
> *To mix with churchyard mould.*

He never visited the young couple again, and they loved one another long and dearly.

J.Á. I 242–5; from Kristrún Ásmundsdóttir (d.1898). This is a variant of AT 470 A, 'The Offended Skull (Statue)', but with the normally tragic ending averted by the bride's cleverness and courage (this brings the story near AT 813 B, where a wife saves her husband from the devil; cf. the role of the heroine in 'The Wizards of the Vestmanna Isles', pp. 169–73). The motif of the huge thigh-bone occurs also in a somewhat similar tale of a girl who, seeing it dug up, remarks 'It would have been fun to kiss that fellow when he was alive'; when the ghost claims a kiss, she gives it boldly, and comes to no harm – or, others say, dares not, and goes mad (J.Á. I 242). The first generations of Icelanders were sometimes thought of as gigantic in later traditions, and the implication is that bones such as these were theirs.

THE MISERLY GHOST

It happened once that the owner of a very fine farm died, but on the very day he died all his money disappeared, and his most valuable goods too – a set of table silver, and many other fine things. Nor could anyone sleep in his bed, for all who did so after his death were themselves found dead next morning. One day, a man came by and asked for a night's lodging; the mistress of the house said it was not possible, and told him what was the matter with this bed, and that she had no other free to offer him to sleep in. The man said he would not be afraid, and insisted on sleeping in that bed, and in the end he got his way.

Towards evening the man goes out to the churchyard, digs up some earth from a grave, and rolls in it till he is muddy all over;

then he goes back and lies down on the bed. At about midnight the door opens, and something peers in and says: 'It's nice and clean in here.' The man feels certain that this must be the dead farmer returning. The ghost now comes right into the room and rips up the floorboards and picks up great quantities of coins from under them, and he tosses them about so that they fall in showers all over him; this goes on and on, far into the night.

When the night is almost over and day will soon be dawning, the man gets out of bed and goes down to the churchyard; there he sees an open grave, and climbs down into it. After a little while the ghost arrives, and asks the man to get out of his grave; but he said he would not, not unless he showed him where he had hidden the valuables which had disappeared at his death. The farmer said he would do no such thing, but in the end he let himself be talked into it, since otherwise he would never manage to get back into his grave.

So then he goes with this man to the wall surrounding his home-field, and rips some turves out of it; there is a trapdoor facing him, and he raises it and goes down into an underground chamber below. The ghost showed the man all the treasures in there, and demanded to be allowed to go back into the grave; but this the man firmly refused, unless he promised never to come out of it again. So then the farmer promised, and they both went back to the grave; the ghost lay down in it, and the living man arranged things there as he thought appropriate.

After this the man goes back to the farm and lies down in the bed; but in the morning when people come to his room, they are all astonished to find him alive. He tells them all about the money and the treasures, and where he found them, and he gets half of it all for himself.

J.Á. I 264–5 (*Apturgángan*); a story current in Skar>sströnd. Ghosts of this type are called *fépúkar* or *maurapúkar*, 'money goblins' or 'ant goblins'. Every night they visit their hoard and play grotesquely with it; as they hate the living, those who wish to spy on them must pretend to be dead men too, e.g. by rubbing themselves with graveyard mould, or wearing ice-cold metal gloves. *Fépúkar* dread daylight so much that they will even abandon their wealth to get back to their graves before dawn. There are four more tales on this theme in J.Á. I 265–70 (one tr. Powell and Magnússon 170–3 and another in Simpson 1988, 102–4), and it also appears as one episode in 'The Boy Who Knew No Fear'. The typical *fépúkar* generally differs from the treasure-haunting ghosts of many other lands by this imbecilic glee over his wealth; the idea of a remorseful, guilt-ridden ghost only too glad to reveal his treasures to anyone bold enough to speak to him is more rarely found in Iceland. Either type of story expresses moral and social condemnation of miserliness, but the Icelandic type adds a powerful undertone of contempt.

THE BOY WHO KNEW NO FEAR

There was once a lad who was a cheeky young dare-devil. All those responsible for him, whether they were his parents or other relations, were very worried over this, for however they handled him they could not teach him to feel scared of anything. When they were forced to give up, they took him to a parish priest who, they thought, would be the best man to have a stern word with the boy and curb his nature. But when the boy came to live with the priest he very soon showed just the same attitude, and could never see any danger in anything, whatever the priest might try. But the boy was never badly behaved or obstinate with him, any more than he had been before with the people at home. And so for some while the boy lived at the priest's, and the priest made every effort to change him somehow, but never succeeded.

One winter day three bodies were brought to the church for burial, but since they arrived late in the day they were left in the church overnight, to be buried next day. It was the custom in those days to bury bodies without coffins, and that was how these were, in shrouds only. When the corpses had been carried in the priest had them laid across the church in the aisle between the pews, one behind the other, with a space between each and the next.

When much of the evening was past, the priest said to the boy: 'Go out to the church for me as fast as you can, my boy, and fetch the book which is on the altar.'

The boy went off quickly, for he was not unco-operative, only reckless. So then he goes out to the church, unlocks it, and means to walk straight in, but as soon as he is a little way in from the door he stumbles over something and falls flat. He is not at all put out, but gropes about in front of him and finds out that he has fallen over a dead body, picks it up and pushes it up on a pew out of his way. He then goes a little further in, and falls over the next body; he deals with it in the same way as the first. Then he goes on again, and falls over the third body, and deals with it as with the others, by taking it out of the aisle and throwing it on a pew. After which, he goes up to the altar, takes the book, locks the church door, and brings the book to the priest.

The priest takes the book, and asks him whether he had noticed anything. The boy said that he had not, and he did not seem in the least dismayed.

The priest said: 'Well now, didn't you notice the corpses in the church, in the aisle? I forgot to warn you about them.'

'Oh yes, the corpses,' said the boy. 'I did notice them, and I wondered what they had to do with you, Father.'

'How did you come to notice them?' says the priest. 'They must have been in your way.'

The boy said: 'I don't reckon they were.'

'How did you manage to get up to the front of the church?' says the priest.

'I pushed them out of the aisle and onto the pews; they're still lying there.'

The priest shook his head, and said no more.

Next morning, when people were up and about, the priest said to the boy: 'You'll have to take yourself off from here; I won't keep you in my household, as you're so reckless that you don't shrink from disturbing the repose of the dead.'

The boy took this calmly, and bade farewell to the priest and his household. After that, he wanders about for some while without a roof over his head; but at one farm where he spent a night, he learnt that the Bishop of Skalholt was dead, so he makes a detour and sets off for Skalholt. By the time he got there night was falling, so he asks for a lodging. The answer was that he was welcome to lodge there, but that he would have to rely on himself alone for protection. He asked whether there was a risk, or what the trouble might be. They answered that things had changed there since the bishop's death, that nobody could bear to stay in the place once darkness fell, and that everyone in the house had had to flee every night since then.

'Then I'm all the better pleased to stay,' said the boy.

Then men told him not to say such things, for it would be no joke to stay. When darkness came they all began to leave the place, and bade the boy farewell with heavy hearts, for they did not expect to see him again. The boy stayed behind, quite cheerful.

When it was quite dark he lit a lamp; then he went round the house, exploring it. Finally he went into the kitchen, where everything was in good order; fat sides of smoked mutton were hanging from the beams, and everything he saw was of the same fine quality. It was a long time since the boy had tasted smoked mutton, and he began to have a longing for it, as he saw such plenty on every side. He did not want to take a nap, so that he should not be caught unawares by the haunting, and so he decides to go and light the fire, chops wood, sets a pot of water on the flames, and cuts up a side of mutton to put in it. So far, he was none the wiser about the haunting. But when everything is in the pot, he hears a muffled voice up the kitchen chimney, saying: 'May I drop in?'

He answers: 'Why shouldn't you drop in?'

At this, down the chimney comes the whole upper part of a man – the head, the shoulders, arms and hands – and this chunk lies on the floor for a while without stirring.

Next, the boy hears the question again from up the kitchen chimney: 'May I drop in?'

He answers as before : 'Why shouldn't you drop in?' Then down the chimney comes the middle part of a man down as far as the legs; this chunk falls beside the first, and lies there just as motionless.

Then once again the boy hears the question from up the kitchen chimney: 'May I drop in?'

He answers as before; 'Why shouldn't you drop in? You need something to stand on.'

Then down came a man's legs, and they were amazingly huge, as also were the sections which had already fallen down the chimney. When these chunks had dropped down, they lay still for a while on the floor.

When the boy grew bored with this state of affairs, he went up to the sections and said: 'Seeing you're all in now, you'd best get moving.'

Then all the sections squirmed up to one another, and joined together to make a mighty huge man. He took no notice of the boy, but walked straight from the kitchen into the house, and the boy followed this big man wherever he went.

The big man goes into one of the main rooms at the front of the house, and goes up to a large chest and opens it, and the boy sees that it is full of coins. Then the big man takes fistful after fistful of coins from the chest and pours them over his head, letting them run all over the floor behind him. He carries on doing this all night till he has emptied the chest; then he takes the heaps he has poured on the floor, and pours coins from them over his head so that they fall inside the chest. The boy stood watching while the ghost poured coins to and fro, and saw how they rolled about in all directions across the floor. Now the ghost starts gathering them together again, flinging coins into the chest and sweeping his hands across the floor to find those which had rolled away from the heap, and the boy realises that he must be thinking how it is getting on for daybreak, and is hurrying as fast as he can.

Now there comes a time when the ghost has got all the coins back in the chest, and the boy thinks he looks as if he's about to leave; indeed, he is just turning to go out from the hall. The boy told him there was no need to be in such a hurry, but the ghost said there was, for day was breaking. The ghost tried to pass him, but the boy caught hold of him, meaning to hinder him. So after a while the ghost grew angry, took a grip on the boy, and said he would not succeed in delaying his departure any longer. The boy grappled with the revenant but soon learnt that he was no match for him, so he avoided coming to grips and only guarded himself against serious injuries and falls. This went on for some time.

At one moment the ghost had his back to the door, which was open, and was about to lift the boy as high as his chest, in order to hurl him down hard. The lad saw what he intended, and knew it would be the death of him. So just as the ghost was gathering all his strength to snatch him up, the boy hurled himself upwards against his chest with such violence that the ghost toppled backwards and lay on his back across the threshold, half in and half out of the room, and the boy landed on top of him as he fell. Now it so happened that when this revenant toppled down with his head outside the door, the light of the sun, which was well above the horizon by then, shone into his eyes, and so he split in half, and the two halves sank into the earth where they lay, one on each side of the threshold, and the ground closed over them when they had disappeared.

Though the boy was rather stiff and bruised after the ghost's attack, he sets to work and makes two wooden crosses which he drives into the ground where the pieces had sunk, one inside and one outside the door of the hall. After this, he lies down and goes to sleep, until the men of the household wake him later in the morning, when it was full day. They greeted him, and now that they saw him alive they were happier than they had been the previous night, and they asked him if he was any the wiser about the nightly haunting of their house. The boy said he had not noticed any haunting. They would not believe him, however much he tried to assure them this was true. After this he stayed there quietly all day, as he was worn out by his encounter with the ghost, and also because the men refused to part with him, as he gave them courage.

That evening when he saw the men about to leave, he tried every means to get them to stay quietly at home, and said they would come to no harm from the haunting. But it was no use; they would not believe him and went off, as they had the night before; but by his words and encouragement he had at least contrived that they parted from him without fear. When they had all left the place, the lad got himself food, lay down to rest, and slept till morning. As soon as the men returned next day they again questioned him about the haunting, but he said he had noticed nothing, and that in future there would be no need to fear anything of the sort. Then he told the whole tale of the previous night, and showed them the crosses on the floor at the spot where the pieces had sunk, and with this he led the men to the treasure chest. They thanked the boy warmly for his courage, and urged him to accept anything they had, either these coins or other money, as a reward for what he had done, and to stay at Skalholt as long as he liked. He thanked them for this fine offer, but said he had no need of wealth or anything else, nor would he stay any longer. However, he stayed one more night, during which all the people stayed in the house too, and no one came to any harm, either then or later.

After this he left Skalholt, much to everyone's regret, and set off in a straight line for the north. There is no more to tell about him for some while, till one day when he came upon a cave. In he went, but he saw twelve beds in a side chamber of the cave, facing one another in two rows of six. These beds were all unmade, and as there was still part of the day left before he need expect the owners of the cave to return, he set to and made all the beds. Having done so, he lay down on the innermost bed of one row, drew the covers carefully over him, and went to sleep.

After a while he is woken by movement in the cave, and hears that many men have come in and are wondering who could have come by and given himself the trouble to make their beds, and they

say they are grateful to him. Then, having eaten, they betake themselves to bed, by what he can make out. But when the one whose
bed he was lying in went to pull the covers back, he at once
noticed the lad. They all thanked him for the good turn he had
done them, and asked him to stay and give them some help about
the home, for they were much in need of it; they were always
obliged to leave the cave at sunrise because otherwise their
enemies would come and fight them there, and so they could never
stay at home. The boy said he would accept their offer, and stay; and
then he enquired how it came about that they had to go off every
day to a battle so stubborn that it never ended. The owners of the
cave said that the other men had been enemies of theirs who had
often done evil in times gone by, and that they, the cave-dwellers,
had always been stronger than them, so that even now they overcame them every evening and killed them. Yet what now happened
was that their enemies always came to life again by the morning,
and every time were more terrible and fierce than the time before,
and that they would undoubtedly slaughter them all inside the cave
if they were not there to face them on the battlefield at sunrise.
After that, they lay down to sleep and slept till morning.

As soon as the sun was up, the men left the cave, well armed, and
told the lad to see to the cave and the housework, which he promised to do. In the course of the day the lad went out to a hazel
wood in the same direction as he had seen them go in the
morning, in order to discover where their meeting place was. As
soon as he had set eyes on the battlefield he ran back to the cave,
after which he makes the beds, sweeps the cave, and does everything necessary. In the evening the owners of the cave came back
weary and worn out, and were glad he had done everything for
them so that they need do nothing but eat and go to bed. So then
they all go to sleep, except the lad; he lies awake, wondering
whether he can find out how it is that their enemies come to life
again by night.

As soon as he thinks his comrades are asleep he gets up, chooses
which of their weapons he prefers, and takes them. Then he goes

to the battlefield, and gets there past midnight. There was nothing to be seen but dead bodies and decapitated heads. He remains there a long time. Towards dawn he sees a mound not far from the battlefield open up; out came a woman wearing a blue cloak and holding a phial. He sees her go straight across the field to where a fallen man lay, and smear something from the phial onto the dead man's headless body, and also onto that part of the neck which was attached to the head, and then set the head back on the trunk, and they at once grew together and the man came back to life. She did the same to two or three others, and they too came alive. Then the boy rushed at the old woman and struck her her death-blow, for now he knew what made the enemies come to life; and after this he slew those she had revived. Once he had done so, he set to work to prove whether he himself could manage to revive the fallen in the same way as the woman, and he smeared stuff from the phial on the stumps, and it worked just as well as before. So now he alternately revived the fallen and slew them again, until the sun came up.

Then his companions from the cave arrived, ready for battle; they had been distressed that he had disappeared, and some of their weapons too. When they arrived, they thought it a very pleasant change that their enemies should all be lying motionless and dead. Seeing the boy there, they greeted him and asked how he happened to be there. Then he told them the whole story, and how the elf-woman had tried to bring all the fallen back to life. He showed them the phial of ointment, took one of the fallen men, smeared ointment on him and put his head back, at which he came alive as fast as ever, but the boy's comrades killed him at once. The men from the cave then thanked him warmly for his courage and invited him to stay with them as long as he liked, and offered him money for his help. He thanked them for their fine offer, and agreed to stay.

After all this, the men from the cave grew so friendly with the boy, and so merry and full of high spirits, that they agreed to find out what it was like to die, since they could all revive one another.

Then they all slew one another and rubbed ointment on, and so came alive again. They got a great deal of fun out of this. On one occasion when the boy's head had been cut off and grafted back on the trunk, his face had been turned backwards and the nape of his neck to the front. Now when the boy caught sight of his own backside, his head being the wrong way round, he almost went crazy with terror, and begged them to free him from such torture by whatever means they could. Then they ran to him and cut his head off again and grafted it back the right way. Then he recovered his wits, and was as fearless as before, and so remained ever after. Then he and his comrades dragged all the dead men's bodies into a heap, piled their weapons on top, and burned them, and with them the elf-woman who had come from the mount with her phial of ointment. After that they went into the mound and took out all the valuable things there, and carried them all back to their cave. The boy stayed with them ever afterwards, and no more tales are told of him.

J.Á. I 270–5; a story current in Reykjavík. Another version is given by Maurer (136–9), where the hero is Björn, nephew of the famous priest and magician Hálfdan Narfason (d. 1568; cf. J.Á. I 515–20); there, owing to the influence of the numerous Master Magician legends, the ghosts are all explained as illusions called up by Halfdan to test the lad. There are also two manuscript versions (Sveinsson 1928, 23). None is as complex in structure as the present version.

The basic pattern is AT 326, 'The Youth Who Wanted to Learn What Fear Is', extremely popular all over Europe; the Icelandic versions are derived from Danish, but in two cases, instead of the normal ending in which the hero learns fear when his wife throws cold water over him or drops a fish down his back, they have the unparalleled finale about the 'men in the cave' and the 'everlasting combat' (see Christiansen 1959, 180–7). These are well-known motifs in Iceland. There are many tales of outlaw bands living in some remote, mysterious spot where outsiders can only come by accident or at the outlaws' own summons; they are some-times called *hellismenn*, 'men of the cave' (J.Á. II 300–4), and in some legends magical powers may be ascribed to them. The second motif, 'everlasting combat', is very old in Scandinavia, and originally mythological; it reappears in fourteenth-century fantastic sagas, notably fiorsteins fláttr uxafóts, where the hero helps one party of dead men against another, since only the living can 'kill' the dead (tr. Simpson, 1965, 218–20), and in Sǫrla fláttr, where the part played here by the old elf-woman is played by a witch-like emissary of the goddess Freyja.

There has been debate as to whether the 'reversed head' joke is an older feature than the 'fish or cold water' joke as a finale to this tale, for it occurs also in Straparola's Italian version of 1550 (see Christiansen 1959, 180–7). It is in any case an idea congenial to Icelandic humour; cf. the story of a girl who, when menaced by a ghost with the words 'Look at my red eyes, how red they are!', overawed it with the retort 'Look at my black arse, how black it is!' (J.Á. I 306).

Other characteristically Icelandic motifs are the coin-tossing of the fépúki, and the wrestling-match, modelled on the famous tussle between Grettir and Glámr.

THE DEACON OF MYRKA

In the old days there was a deacon living at Myrka in Eyjafjord, but what his name was is not said. He had as his mistress a woman named Gudrun, who lived, so some people say, at Bægisa, on the other side of Horga River, where she was servant to a priest. The deacon had a grey-maned horse which he always rode; he called it Faxi.

One day, a little before Christmas, the deacon went to Bægisa to invite Gudrun to the Christmas festivities at Myrka, and he promised her that he would come and fetch her in due course and take her to the festivities on Christmas Eve. For several days before the deacon went over to give Gudrun this invitation, there had been heavy snows and hard frosts; but on the very day he rode to Bægisa there came a sudden thaw, and the ice broke up, so that by the end of the day the river had grown impassable by reason of floating ice and a strong current, while the deacon meanwhile loitered at Bægisa. When he did set out, he never gave a thought to how the weather had changed in the course of the day, but assumed that the river was still frozen solid. He crossed the smaller stream in Yxnadal by a strip of ice that still held, but when he got to the Horga River, it had cleared itself of ice. So he rides downstream till he comes to Saurbœ, the next farm below Myrka, where the ice still held. The deacon rides out onto the strip of ice, but just when he is half way across, it breaks under him, and he fell into the river.

Next morning, when the farmer at the neighbouring farm of Thufnavellir got out of bed, he sees a saddled and bridled horse by his homefield, and thinks he recognises it as the deacon's Faxi. He is taken aback, for he had seen the deacon ride away the day before, but had not noticed him return, and so he soon suspected what must have happened. He goes down to the homefield; and, just as he had thought, it was Faxi there, soaking wet and in a sorry state. Next, he goes down to a small headland that juts into the river, and there he finds the deacon washed up on shore dead. The farmer at once brings this news to Myrka. Now when the deacon was found, the back of his head had been badly cut about by floating ice. Anyway, he was carried home to Myrka and buried, during the week before Christmas.

From the time the deacon left Bægisa right up to Christmas Eve no news of what had happened could reach Bægisa from Myrka, because of the breaking up of the ice and the flooding. But on Christmas Eve the weather was calm, and the river had gone down during the night, so Gudrun was looking forward to the festivities at Myrka. Towards evening she went to get ready, and when she was in the middle of dressing she heard a knock; another woman who was with her went to the door, but saw nobody – for indeed it was neither clear nor dark outside, as clouds were driving fast across the moon, sometimes hiding it and sometimes not. When this girl came in again and said she had seen nothing, Gudrun said: 'It must be a joke meant for me, so of course I must go.' By then she was quite ready, except that she still had to put her riding-cape on. She picked up the cape and put one arm in its sleeve, but simply slung the other side over her shoulder and held it.

As soon as she came out she saw Faxi standing by the door, and beside him a man whom she took to be the deacon. They did not say one word to each other, so it is said. He lifted her and set her on the horse's back, and himself mounted in front of her. So then they rode on for a while, without speaking. They came to the River Horga, where ice was still piled high along the banks; and as the horse leapt down from the ice into the water, the deacon's hat was jerked forward, and Gudrun saw the skull itself laid bare.

At that very moment the moon came out from behind the clouds, and the deacon spoke:

> *The moon glides,*
> *And Death rides;*
> *Don't you see a patch of white*
> *On this head of mine tonight,*
> *Garun, Garun?*

She was startled, and remained silent. But other people say Gudrun herself lifted his hat from behind, and then said: 'I see what there is to see.'

There is no mention of any further talk between them, nor of their journey, until they reached Myrka; there they dismounted at the lychgate of the churchyard, and the deacon said to Gudrun:

> *You wait here, Garun, Garun,*
> *While I take my Faxi, Faxi,*
> *To the field beyond the fence.*

So saying, he went off with the horse. She happened to look into the churchyard, and there she saw an open grave; she was horribly frightened, but even so, hitting on a plan, she clutches the rope of the lychgate bell. At once she is clutched from behind, and it proved lucky for her that she had only had time to put one arm through the sleeve of her cape, for the tugging was so fierce that the cape tore at the seam of the sleeve, and the last she saw of the deacon was that he tumbled into the open grave, still holding her torn cape in his hand, and the earth poured down onto him from both sides.

As for Gudrun, she rang without stopping till the farm people from Myrka came out and found her, for she was so frightened at all this that she dared not leave the spot nor stop ringing, for she felt sure she had been dealing with the deacon's ghost, even though no word of his death had yet reached her. And she no longer had the least doubt of it once she had had a talk with the people of Myrka, who told her all about the deacon's death, while she in return told them of her experience. That same night, as soon as everyone was in bed and the lights were out, the deacon came and attacked Gudrun, and this caused such turmoil that the people had to get up again, and nobody got any sleep that night. For two weeks after that she could not bear to be ever alone, and someone had to sit up with her every night. Some say a priest had to sit on the edge of her bed and read psalms.

Now a magician was sent for, from Skagafjord in the west. As soon as he came, he made them dig up a large rock from above the homefield and roll it up against the gable-wall of the house. In the evening, when it grew dusk, the deacon comes and tries to get into the house, but the magician forces him back to the gable-wall, and there drives him down into the ground by mighty incantations; he then rolls the rock on top of him, and there the deacon has been forced to stay to this day. After this, all the haunting stopped, and Gudrun grew more cheerful. A little later she went home to Bægisa, but people say she was never the same again.

J.Á. I 280–3, from Ingibjörg Þorvaldsdóttir (b.1807), with additional details from the Revd Páll Jónsson (d.1889). The latter's version is translated in Kvideland and Sehmsdorf, 92–3, and in Simpson 1988, 106–9. A fine version of the international type AT 365, 'The Dead Bridegroom Carries off his Bride' (also known as 'Lenore', from the title of Bürger's ballad). Four other Icelandic versions are known, one attached to a different pair of farms, and the others unlocalised (J.Á. I 283, 283–4; Maurer 73; Sveinsson 1928, 33). These four all depart from the international prototype in explaining the ghost's behaviour as revenge by a rejected lover, this appearing more credible than motiveless malignity. All five Icelandic versions agree that the girl escaped and the ghost was laid; a rock at Myrka was believed, in the late eighteenth century, to be that under which the ghost was pinned (J.Á. I 283). This story, therefore, like several others in the present section, can be regarded also as a variant of ML 4021*, 'A Troublesome Ghost Laid'.

A detail in the present version reflecting Icelandic beliefs is the ghost's use of 'Garún', a non-existent name, instead of 'Gu>rún', because ghosts are unable to utter the word *Gu>*, 'God'. Another is the knock at the door; after dark, Icelanders would tap the window, and a knock, especially if it were only a single stroke, was a sure sign of a ghost or other evil creature seeking entry (J.Á. II 542, and cf. 'The Bridegroom and the Dead Man', pp. 131–5). Finally, although a verse referring to the moon and the ride of the dead is a common feature in AT 365, the present narrative adds the precise detail of the clouds suddenly clearing; this is yet another reminiscence of the fight between Grettir and Glámr, at the climax of which the saga-writer makes a similarly eerie use of scudding clouds and intermittent moonlight – indeed, the identical phrase is used at this point in both saga and tale.

THE GHOST'S SON

At one time, long ago, the farm of Bakki (now called Prestsbakki) in Hrutafjord stood further north on a hill by the sea called Hellisholar. But later it was moved because it was haunted, and was rebuilt where it is now.

It happened that a farmer in the parish had asked for the hand of the daughter of the priest at Bakki, but did not get her; this put him in such a rage that he fell ill and died, and was buried in Bakki churchyard. This happened one summer, and much of the winter passed without anything noteworthy happening, except that people thought the priest's daughter seemed rather strange that winter.

One evening it happened that her foster-mother, an old woman who knew a great deal, went out to the churchyard with her knitting; the weather was fine, and clouds were driving fast across the moon. The priest's daughter had told her that this man came to her each night and treated her lovingly and tenderly. She said she had become weary of his frequent visits, and that she found now that she was pregnant by him; also, she said that he had said that this child would be unlucky in years to come. So then she had asked her foster-mother to help her in her trouble, and therefore the old woman went out to the churchyard, as we have already said.

The woman went to the man's grave, and it was open. She dropped her ball of wool into the grave, sat down on the edge of it, and stayed there knitting. Now ghosts cannot get back into their graves if anyone drops anything into them, and the old woman knew this, which was why she dropped her ball in. So there she sat and waited until the ghost came. He told her to take the ball out of his grave, so that he could lie down in it. She said she would do no such thing until he agreed to tell her the reasons for his night wanderings.

The ghost said he went visiting the priest's daughter – 'And her father can't stop me now,' says he. 'I've given her a child, and it is a boy she is carrying.'

'Tell me what lies in store for the child,' says the old woman.

'This is what lies in store for the boy,' says the ghost. 'He will become the priest here at Bakki, and the first time he ever stands in front of the altar and blesses the congregation, the church and everyone inside it will sink into the ground. And I will then think my revenge is complete, for not having had the priest's daughter while I was alive.'

'Yours is a fearful prophecy, if it proves true,' says the old woman. 'Is there any way of preventing or averting these horrors?'

'There is one way,' says the ghost, 'if someone were to stab the priest before the altar just as he was about to bless the people. But no one would do that.'

'Do you stick to that?' says she. 'Is there no other way to stop this misfortune?'

'No, no other way,' says the ghost.

'Then down you go into your grave,' says she, 'and never come up out of it again!'

She then took out her ball of wool and the ghost went down into the grave, which closed itself. The old woman read such spells over the grave that there was never any sign of haunting again. She went home, and told no one what had passed.

So time went by, and the priest's daughter gave birth to a boy, a big handsome one. It is not said that she ever told her father who the baby's father was; and the boy grew up at Bakki with his mother and grandfather. One could soon see that this lad outshone the rest in both mind and body; when he grew older he was sent to study, and always seemed to outstrip everyone else. So time went on till his training was finished and he became his grandfather's curate.

Now, to go back to the girl's old foster-mother. She saw that things could not go on as they were, for if so, what the ghost had told her long ago would come true. So she went to her son, who was a very brave man and would not have too many scruples when there was much at stake. She told him the whole story, and earnestly urged him to kill the new priest as soon as he turned round to bless the congregation from the altar, and said she would answer for it that no harm would come of it if he did. He was unwilling, but since his mother was so distressed and begged him so earnestly he promised in the end, and she made him swear not to change his mind.

Now the day came when the young priest was to say his first Mass, and great crowds came to the church, and they all admired his elegance and his voice. But as he raised his hand to bless the congregation, the old woman made a sign to her son. He stood up, though it was much against his will, and stabbed the priest to the heart, and he fell dead. This took everybody quite by surprise, and they wanted to take the slayer. But some men went to see if they could help the priest, but there was nothing left of him at all, except for the topmost vertebra of his spine, which lay on the step in front of the altar. So they now saw that there was more to this man than met the eye. Then the old woman stepped forward and told the whole story from the beginning, at which they were all filled with terror, and thanked her for her resourcefulness and courage. They also noticed then that the church was tilted, and that the chancel had sunk a little way into the ground; this was because the priest had managed to intone the first word of the blessing before he was killed.

After this, Bakki was so haunted that the farm was moved, and rebuilt where it stands now.

J.Á. I 285–7 (*Bakkadraugurinn*); a story current in Hrútafjör>ur. For two variants, see J.Á. I 287–9 and Maurer 300–1; in both, the priest is killed by his altar-server, and three drops of blood, not a bone, remain. The story is related to the Irish AT 764, 'The Devil's Son as Priest', in which a devil or a dead man predicts that a quarrelling couple will have a son, whose true father will be himself, that he will grow up to be a priest, and that all whom he then sprinkles with holy water will be damned. But the young priest, learning his true nature, is saved from this curse by severe penances.

The idea that a vertebra alone remains when a ghost has been stabbed belongs properly to the stories about 'Sendings', for which see 'The Vertebra' below, pp.167–8. The ball of wool in the grave can be paralleled in a legend from the Isle of Lewis in the Hebrides, in which a woman prevents a ghost from re-entering his grave by laying her spindle across it, and so forces him to answer her questions (Swire 1961, 113; cf. MacDonald, 65. See also Hallfre>ur Örn Eiriksson, 'Some Icelandic Ghost Fabulates', *Arv* 49 (1992), 117–22).

The Girl who Turned in her Grave

On a farm in the western district of Alptamyra, in the nineteenth century, there lived two brothers and a sister; here was nobody but themselves to work on the farm. Now, their lands lay in such a way that they had to cross a certain fjord or bay in order to reach their meadows. One evening as they were all three returning from their meadows, they ferried a load of hay across with them, and they had loaded the boat so fully that there was nowhere for the girl to sit except right at the stern, while the two brothers rowed on the same bench amidships, where there was a clear space, but they could not see their sister because of the pile of hay. In this manner they crossed the fjord, and came to land at the most convenient spot. But as soon as they went to unload the boat, they found that the girl had disappeared, and they did not know what had become of her, except that they assumed that she had fallen overboard. As the evening had grown very dark, so that one could barely see in front of one's face, they took no steps to search for her, being certain that she would never be found alive.

So they went home, and slept. That night, one of the brothers dreamed of her; he thought that she came to him in his sleep and showed him where to look for her. Next morning the brothers both went out in the boat to search, and they drew her body from the water at the very spot which she herself had pointed out in the dream. After this, she was made ready for burial, and laid to rest in the churchyard.

Now it so happened that this girl had been in love with a man in that neighbourhood, but he had refused to take any notice of her. When they were about to bury her, this man started having nightmares about her, and he complained of this. Not long afterwards, this same man disappeared one day, and nobody knew what had become of him. So then a band of men went out to look for him, and he was found down on the beach at the foot of some high cliffs, all battered and crushed. The general assumption was that the girl must have walked, and must have thrown him over the cliff, and so killed him. As soon as this rumour reached them, her brothers went and dug her up, and when they opened the coffin they saw that there was indeed something wrong, for the girl had turned round inside it, and was now lying face down. They did not like the look of this at all, so at the same time as they turned her the right way round in the coffin, they also drove two sharp steel nails into the soles of her feet, and so closed the coffin up again and went home, leaving everything as it should be. After this, there was no more sign that their sister went wandering about.

J.Á. I 298 (*Stúlkan í Álptamyrarsókn*), from Jón Borgfir>ingur, from a story current in Ísafjör>ur. For other tales of ghosts revealing in dreams where their corpses lie, see J.Á. I 228–32. The nails in the feet used here to lay the ghost are paralleled by the broken needle in the story quoted in the note to 'Isn't it Fun in the Dark!' (p.122), and also by the widespread custom in many lands of staking the corpses of vampires, suicides, and other suspected revenants.

THE WOMAN IN THE RED CAP

In one priest's household there lived an elderly woman as a pensioner. She often used to quarrel with the servants there, and one of them, whose name was Jon, would play spiteful tricks on her. She promised him, shortly before her death, that she would take revenge on him for the way he had treated her. Soon after the old woman's death, Jon died out on the fells, but his body was not found till much later; it was then buried, but the very next night the grave was opened and the coffin smashed. So his body was buried a second and a third time, but the same thing always happened, so that it could not lie still in the grave. Then the priest found a way out, by having the body put in a sack and left to lie behind the church door.

Now some time passed, until one day one of the women who worked on the priest's farm, whose name was Gudrun, lost her tobacco pouch. That evening she started making such a fuss over her loss that the priest finally offered to give her a new pouch, and some tobacco in it too, if she would go out to the church then and there, and fetch the sack of bones. She did not turn a hair, but just went and fetched the sack.

That night Jon appeared to her, and said: 'You have treated my bones badly, and you will have to make me full amends for that. Be sure to go out to the church on New Year's Eve, and say to the woman in the red cap: "Forgive the skeleton that lies behind the door."'

Gudrun did as she was asked; on New Year's Eve she went out to the church, and it was full of people, but she took no notice of that. There among the rest was a woman in a red cap; Gudrun went up to her and said exactly what she had been told to say. In a harsh voice, the woman answered 'Yes.' Next morning Gudrun told the whole story to the priest. Then Jon's bones were buried once more, and after this the grave was not disturbed again.

J.Á. I 306–7, from Maurer 74–5. For two variants, see J.Á. I 305–8; one is tr. in Powell and Magnússon, 235–7. This is a sub-type of ML 4020 'The Unforgiven Skeleton', a story popular in all three Scandinavian countries, but with wide variation in detail (for the Danish and Swedish sub-types, see Ellekilde and von Sydow in *Nordisk Kultur* IXB, 1931, 149–50, 232; for the Norwegian, Christiansen 1958). In the Aarne-Thompson system these tales are classified as AT 760, 'The Unquiet Grave'; there is also the closely similar AT 882B★, 'The Forgiven Skeleton', from Czechoslovakia.

The Icelandic story differs from most versions at AT 760 (= ML 4020), but resembles AT 882B★, in that the forgiveness must be obtained from someone dead, not from a living person or a priest. The idea of hostility between two of the dead is familiar to Icelandic thought (cf. J.Á. I 226), but that of a guilty person condemned to expiate a crime after death is not. The encounter in the church on New Year's Eve is based on the common belief that on that night 'the churchyard rises', i.e. the dead go to church, in the clothes they were buried in, to hear a midnight Mass there; they are followed by the fetches of all those in the parish who will die during the next year (J.Á. I 223). This belief forms the basis of ML 4015 'The Midnight Mass of the Dead', about a living woman who unwittingly attends this ghostly service; this legend, common throughout Scandinavia and in many parts of Europe, clearly influenced the final episode of the present tale.

MORI, THE GHOST OF IRAFELL

There was a man called Kort Thorvardson, a high official and a respected farmer; for a long time he lived at Modruvellir in Kjos, but eventually moved to Flekkudal, where he died in 1821. He was twice married; his first wife was called Ingibjorg, and her family came from the north. Many men had wanted to marry her before Kort, but she had refused them all. Her former admirers thought they had been very shabbily treated when Kort married her, even though he was far above them in many ways, and this made them so bitter that they paid a wizard from the north to send a Sending against Kort and his wife. In order to make this, the wizard used a little boy who, so the story goes, had died of exposure in the open country; the wizard called him back while he was still warm, or even not quite dead, and sent him against Kort and his wife at Modruvellir, and decreed that this ghost would attach itself to them and to their descendants to the ninth generation, and do them great harm.

People who have seen this ghost (and they are by no means few) describe him as wearing grey breeches and a russet cloak over his jacket, and a black hat with a very broad brim; there is a deep gash or tear in the brim above his left eye. He takes his name from the russet [*mór*] cloak, and so is called Mori. The wizard's decree has been fulfilled only too well, so they think, for as soon as Mori came south he attacked Modruvellir, as planned, and did much harm of various sorts to Kort and his wife, killing their livestock and spoiling their food. But there are no instances of Mori killing people directly, neither at first nor later.

Once, Kort and his wife had reared two calves through the winter. Mori chased them both over a rock-cliff next summer, and they were found dead at the foot. Another time, Kort had a mare, and this mare and her foal had been allowed to graze all summer in his home-pastures. Late that summer, men saw the foal galloping round and round a rock as if it had gone crazy, and then it fell dead. When they got to it, the foal was lying dead; it had the end of its gut stuck fast to the rock, and had torn all its own guts out, and then fallen dead. This was blamed on Mori.

Since Mori had not been quite thoroughly dead when he was called back, he, like other such ghosts, needed his food. Therefore he had to be given his rations, as for every man in the household, both at Modruvellir and later on when he took up residence at Irafell to haunt Kort's son Magnus; food meant for him had always to be set out in a particular place. Mori had made sure of this by turning everything topsy-turvy in Ingibjorg's dairy; sometimes he would sit on the cross-beams of the dairy and dabble about in the milk churns with his paws, or he would fling them on the floor and splash the curds all over Ingibjorg herself or up as high as the rafters, or else he would throw turf and gravel into the dairy-food where it stood ready, and so ruin it. To counter this, Ingibjorg hit on the plan of giving him his ration of dairy-food at each meal, after which he spoilt it far less. However, on one occasion it did happen that Mori's supper ration was forgotten. Next morning when people went into the dairy they saw him sitting there; he had his great paws right down inside each barrel of curds, and was squatting across the rims of both barrels at once, so that he could paddle in the curds and splash them about at the same time. After that, they took care never to forget to give him his share.

But it wasn't only food that Mori needed; he was also believed to need sleep, just like anybody else, and it is said that after he went to haunt Magnus Kortsson at Irafell, Magnus always had to leave an empty bed for him just opposite his own bed, and that no one but Mori dared sleep in it. Once, at the autumn sheep-gathering, it happened that many people came to Irafell and were given hospitality for the night. Late that evening a boy arrived and asked to be put up. Magnus said he was welcome to use the house, but that he could not offer him any place to sleep except the floor, unless he was willing to lie on the bed opposite his own – and this the boy accepted thankfully. When he lies down he falls asleep quickly, but no sooner is he asleep than something frightful comes over him, and there is a rattling in his throat; he wakes with a start, and all night long he can't get a moment's quiet rest for these attacks. Next day the weather was so bad that the guests could not leave, and so stayed a second night at Irafell. That evening some lads who lived at Irafell and knew Mori pretty well, having had plenty of mudslinging matches against him, took a hand in the game; they stuck knives all round the bed with their points sticking out through the boards on every side. That night the boy slept quietly, and people thought it was owing to the fact that Mori did not dare go near him because of the pointed knives.

After Kort died in 1821, Mori at first attached himself to his eldest son Magnus, who lived for a long time at Irafell (as has been mentioned already), and as Mori haunted that farm for so long he was nicknamed Mori of Irafell, and the name has stuck to him ever since. There is a story told about Magnus, that he once went down to Seltjarness when there were large shoals of fish off shore there, and since he had no regular place on board anyone's boat he went from boat to boat and got a place in a different one each day. Two days running he got a seat in the boat of Sigurd of Hrolfsskali; but then Sigurd's rowers began to notice that Magnus was never alone, wherever he went. And so on the third morning when Magnus went aboard and Sigurd and his men were already afloat, the rowers spoke their mind about Mori; indeed, it is said that they had seen something looking like a ball of russet wool or a dry horse-turd come rolling up on board with Magnus. At this, Sigurd, who was held to be a wary and intelligent man, told Magnus to leave the boat, for he would not take him out to sea again – either because he himself had also seen some sign of Mori, or because he did not want his rowers to distrust Magnus and blame him for their bad luck if anything went wrong.

On one occasion Magnus of Irafell left some loose sheets of 'Hallgrim's Psalms' with Asgeir Finnbogason, who at that time lived at Bradrædi, for them to be bound up. One evening Asgeir was out, and his wife waited up for him; and at first she was up and about, but later she got into bed, and merely stayed awake with a light burning till Asgeir came home. Then he too went to bed, and so they put the light out. Then she saw a rough-looking figure come into the house, sit on a chair by the bed, and lay one arm along the bed-board; now she was lying on the outer side of the bed, and she found this arm so heavy and bulky that she called out and asked who it was, and whether it was their foster-son Jon. There was no reply. She again asked who had come in, and told him to take himself off to the lowest pit of Hell. Then up stands the man who had been sitting on that chair, and his cat's eyes glint in the moonlight that shone through the window; then he vanished, through the locked door. Then there came a terrific loud crash, and at the same moment down falls a shelf on the far side of the room, in the corner opposite the bed; there were many books standing on it, among others the sheets of 'Hallgrim's Psalms' which Asgeir had taken from Magnus to bind. On top of the shelf were several pairs of cups, and these were smashed to bits, as one can imagine, and the pieces rolled all over the floor. After this, the mistress of the house had the lamp relit, and got someone to sit up by her all night, and did not get much sleep. But next day, early in the morning, Magnus himself arrived at Bradrædi to ask for the loose sheets which had been lying on the shelf – and he was told what a pleasant ghost he had as his companion!

Once, another of Kort's sons, named Einar, set out from home to go to Kjos to see some kinsmen there. It was in early winter. Einar went by the coast road across Kollafjord and up onto Kjalarnes, but by the time he got there dusk was falling. He went on all the same, and came to Skrautholar on Kjalarnes after bed-time; he was no stranger to that household, but all the same he did not want to be a nuisance and rouse everyone, when they had just fallen asleep, so he decided to go and look in the cowhouse and see if he could find himself a space to lie there for the night. When he comes into the cowhouse, he finds one stall empty, lies down, and sleeps till morning. In the morning he gets up early, goes to find the people of the house, and says he hopes they do not mind the fact that he made himself at home, went into the cowhouse, and spent the night in the empty stall, as he had not wanted to be a nuisance. The men of the house said he could have come in, and welcome too, even if he had woken them; and that his coming in the way he did had been far worse for them, because on the very morning of the day he came, their best cow had been found lying with her neck broken in the same stall where he later lay, and that it looked as if Mori, who followed him and all Kort's children, had decided to make room for his master when he was due to pass that way, in case he needed to use the cow-stall, as had indeed happened now.

Selected from J.Á. I 378–88, from local traditions. Ghosts who attach themselves for long periods to particular families or farms are called *fylgidraugar* or *fylgjur*, 'followers'; they are always malevolent, and all illnesses and afflictions in the family they 'follow', or indeed among their neighbours, were often ascribed to them. (This usage contrasts with other senses of the word *fylgja*: in the older sagas, a benevolent guardian spirit, often in animal form; in later lore, the 'fetch' of a living man, or the afterbirth. See J.Á. I 354–9). They resembled some of the more sinister British brownies and boggarts in their poltergeist tricks, and in requiring offerings of food; but they were far from being helpful spirits, their rare attempts in that line being apt to turn out disastrously, as in the case of Mori and the cow-stall.

Fylgidraugar can be either male or female; they are generally thought to be either a Sending, as this Mori was, or the vengeful ghost of someone ill-used by some member of the family they haunt. Male ones are very often called Mori because of their russet jackets (dark unbleached woollen clothes being a mark of poverty); a few are called Lalli or Goggur. Female ones are called Skotta, 'Peaky', because they wear the old-fashioned tall coif, but with the peak turned backwards like a dangling tail; they also sometimes drool and suck their fingers. There is a host of tales of such ghosts in J.Á. I 361–404. The belief in them was widespread in the eighteenth century, and still strong in the nineteenth; Jón Árnason brings his ten-page account of the misdeeds of Mori of Irafell down to his own time with a reference to Einar Kortsson's youngest daughter. Indeed, modern collectors have found that the belief in certain Moris and Skottas survived into the twentieth century, though more rarely.

5

BLACK MAGIC

How to Raise the Dead

There are many tales about dead men whom those skilled in magic have brought back to life and forced to do them service. Some say that to do this one must take one bone from a dead man and put magic strength into it so that it takes on human shape, and then send it to attack those one wants to harm. If the man against whom such a Sending is sent is clever enough to strike precisely the bone inside it which had been taken from the dead body, or to name it by its right name, the ghost will not be able to do anything to him and will have to leave him alone.

But others say that more than this is needed to raise a ghost. First, one must see that it is done on the night between a Friday and a Saturday, and preferably between either the 18 and 19 or the 28 and 29 of a month; but which month or which week it is does not matter. The sorcerer who means to raise a ghost must, on the previous evening, write the Our Father backwards on paper or parchment with a water-rail's quill, using his own blood, drawn from his left arm. He must also carve certain runes on a stick, and go out to the churchyard at midnight, taking both paper and stick, and go to whichever grave he chooses – but it is thought prudent to pick out one of the smaller ones. He must lay the stick on the grave and roll it to and fro, meanwhile chanting the Our Father backwards from his paper, and also certain formulas which few people know.

Then little by little the grave begins to stir, and various strange sights appear to the sorcerer while the dead man is being very gradually raised; but it goes very slowly, as the dead are most unwilling to move, and say 'Let me lie quiet!' But the wizard must not give in to their pleading, nor yet let himself be dismayed by the sights, but mutter his incantations faster than ever and roll the stick, until the dead man is half out of the ground. At the same time he must be very careful that no earth falls outside the grave when it begins to heave, for such earth can never be put in again.

When the dead man has risen half way out, he must ask him two questions (not three, or he will sink down again out of fear of the Trinity); the usual ones are who he was in his lifetime, and how powerful a man he then was. Others say there was one question only, namely: 'How old are you?' If the ghost says he died as a middle-aged man or older, it is not thought safe to proceed any further, because at a later stage the sorcerer will have to wrestle with the ghost, and ghosts can be extremely strong, their strength being half as great again as it was in life, and so proportionate to their age. That is why sorcerers prefer to raise children of about twelve to fourteen, or at any rate people who are not over thirty, and never on any account those older than themselves.

When the dead man has said who he is and is half way out of the grave, the sorcerer can either drive him down again if he chooses, or can continue the spells till he is quite out. When the dead first emerge from their graves, their mouths and nostrils are all bubbling with a frothy mixture of mucus and mud known as 'corpse-froth'; this the wizard licks off with his own tongue. Then he must draw blood from under the little toe of his right foot, and moisten the ghost's tongue with it. Some say that as soon as he has done so the ghost attacks him, and he will need all his strength to get him under; if he succeeds and the ghost falls, then the latter is henceforth bound to serve the wizard in every way; but if the ghost is the stronger, he will drag the man down into the grave with him – and those who thus come into a ghost's power never return again. But others say that it is the sorcerer who attacks the ghost when he is only half way up, forcing him onto his back while his legs are still caught fast and keeping him there until he is ready to lick his mouth and nostrils and moisten his tongue.

Now if for any reason the sorcerer chooses not to let the ghost come more than half way, and prefers to send him down again, it is usually enough to speak the name of the Trinity or to say the Our Father the right way round; but if the dead man was himself a wizard in his lifetime, more than this is needed. The sorcerer must have with him a cord to which he has tied the ropes of both the bells on the lych-gate (or all of them if there are more than two, since otherwise the dead man would seize the rope that was still free and ring that bell in opposition to the sorcerer, so that no magic rhymes or formulas could touch him). So while wizards are getting rid of ghosts, they ring the bells without stopping, and recite not only the Our Father but also certain magic rhymes, very different from those used to raise them. If the sorcerer does not send the ghost down again, it will follow him and his descendants for nine generations. So too do ghosts that have finished the tasks their raisers first gave them, unless the sorcerers send them on other errands or manage to get rid of them – and he is a good wizard who can do this without danger! For some say ghosts get stronger and stronger for the first forty years they are above ground, stay unchanged for the next forty, and dwindle away during the third forty; they do not normally remain active any longer, unless some spell or word of power causes them to do so.

J.Á. I 317–19; this and other passages of Jón Árnason's work that are descriptive rather than narrative are collations of information from many persons, and no individual informant is named.

Belief in necromancy has a long history in Iceland; it was particularly associated with the cult of Ó>inn, and was closely linked to his function as the god of esoteric wisdom. The necromancers of later legend were less concerned with wisdom and prophetic power, although one, fiorlei-fur fiór>arson (d. 1647), is said to have kept a dead man's head in a chest or in a rock cleft, to prophesy for him (J.Á. I 523). In most tales, the necromancer is purely vicious; he raises the dead simply in order to send them to attack his enemies or plague them by perpetual hauntings. A ghost so used is called a Sending; it can take on several forms, as the following stories will show. The earliest instance of a Sending is the 'wooden man' made from driftwood and a human heart in the fourteenth-century fiorleifs fláttr jarlaskálds (tr. Simpson, 1965, 141–52). The belief in this and other forms of black magic reached their fullest development in the seventeenth century and the first half of the eighteenth (cf. Benedikz 1964, Daví>sson 1940–43; Simpson 1975). For some English examples of the magical uses of corpses, skulls, bones, and graveyard mould, see Thomas 231 and 443 and references given there; also Briggs 1971, I 434–6.

THE VERTEBRA

A farmer was once out in his stack-yard when the day was almost done and the light was fading fast. He noticed something coming into the yard, and all at once he felt afraid of it, so he hastily flung down his pitchfork and ran away. However, as he had to feed his cattle, he came back shortly after to look for his pitchfork. He finds it, and on the prong of it is a single vertebra from a man's body.

The farmer realises now that it must have been a ghost that came into the yard, for he knew, from what learned men say, that one need have no more than a single human bone in order to make a ghost of it by magic, and that if a man could contrive to strike this bone with an iron point, the ghost would be defeated. The farmer thought his shot had been an incredibly lucky one, for it had been done by pure instinct. He took the pitchfork with the vertebra on it and kept them both carefully.

J.Á. I 320–1, from the Revd Sveinbjörn Gu>mundsson, c.1847. This belief well exemplifies the essentially physical quality of Icelandic ghosts; even when the corpse as a whole is absent, there must be at least one bone. Besides this and the following tale, see the anecdote of how fiorleifur fiór>arson (d.1647) drove away a ghost by stabbing it (J.Á. I 523). In Iceland as elsewhere, iron is effective against evil creatures.

THE NECKBONE ON THE KNIFE

A certain widow lived on a farm of her own in the north country. She was well off and very capable, so several people asked for her hand, and among others a fellow in the same neighbourhood who was skilled in wizardry – and him she refused. This widow had the second sight, which made it easier for her to protect herself.

Not long after, she was in the larder one day towards evening, preparing food rations for her household, and she was slicing a black pudding. She saw a spectre making its way in along the passage, and in it came by the larder door. The woman stood there with the knife in her hand, and faced the spectre resolutely and fearlessly. The spectre hesitated and tried to pass to one side of the woman, or behind her, for an unclean spirit never attacks a fearless person from in front. The woman saw that the spectre was quite black, except that it had one white mark. She drove her knife into that spot; there was a loud crash, and the woman lost her grip on the knife, just as if it had been jerked out of her hand. She saw nothing more, and she could not find her knife.

Next morning the knife was found out on the flagged court; the top vertebra from a man's back was stuck on the point of it, and yet all the gates had been closed the previous evening.

J.Á. I 321, from the Revd Skúli Gíslason (d.1888).

THE WIZARDS OF THE VESTMANNA ISLES

When the Black Death was raging in Iceland, eighteen wizards gathered, swore friendship with one another, and sailed out to the Vestmanna Isles, intending to ward off death there as long as they could. As soon as they saw by their secret arts that the sickness was abating on the mainland, they wanted to find out whether anyone there was still alive; so they agreed to send one of their company to the mainland, and for this errand they chose one who was neither the most nor the least skilled in their arts. They ferried him to land, and told him that if he was not back before Christmas they would send him a Sending which would kill him. This was early in Advent.

The man went off, walked a long way, and wandered far and wide. But nowhere did he see a living soul; farms stood open, and dead bodies lay about, scattered here and there. Finally he came to one farm whose doors were shut. He was amazed, and now hope stirred in him that he might find some living man. He knocked, and out came a young and pretty girl. He greeted her, but she flung her arms round his neck and wept for joy to see a man, for she said she had thought there was nobody left alive but her. She asked him to stay with her, and he agreed. So now they went indoors and talked; she asked him where he had come from, and where he was going. He told her, and also told her that he would have to be back before Christmas, but all the same she asked him to stay with her as long as he could, and he was so sorry for her that he promised that he would. She told him there was nobody alive in those parts, for she said she had walked a whole week's journey from her house in each direction, and found no one.

Now time slipped by and Christmas drew near, and then the man from the islands wanted to go. The girl begged him to stay, and said that his friends would not be so hard-hearted as to make him pay for it if he stayed with her when she was left all alone in the world. So he let himself be persuaded.

And now Christmas Eve had come, and now he is determined to go, whatever she may say. So then she sees that it's no good pleading any longer, and says: 'Do you really think you can get out to the islands tonight? Don't you think you might just as well die here beside me as die somewhere on the way?'

The man realised that the time was too short now, and resigned himself to stay quietly there and wait for death where he was. So the night passed, and he was very gloomy, but the girl was as merry as could be, and asked whether he could see how the men on the Isles were getting on. He said that they were preparing to send a Sending ashore, and that it would arrive that day. Now the girl sat down on the bed beside him, while he lay in bed, a little way behind her. He said that he was beginning to grow sleepy, and that this was due to the Sending's onslaught. Then he fell asleep. The girl sat at the foot of the bed, and she would constantly rouse him a little and make him tell her where the Sending now was. But the nearer it came the deeper he slept, and finally, just after saying that the Sending had reached her farm-lands, he fell into such a deep sleep that she could not wake him again – nor was it long before she saw a russet vapour come into the farmhouse.

This vapour glided gently, very gently, up the room towards her, and then took on human shape. The girl asks the Sending where it is going, and it tells her what its errand is, and tells her to get up off the bed – 'for I can't get at him on account of you,' it says.

The girl says that in that case it will have to do something for her. The Sending asks what that might be. The girl says it is to let her see how huge it could make itself. The Sending agrees to this, and now it grows so huge that it fills the whole house.

Then the girl says: 'Now I want to see how small you can make yourself.'

The Sending says it can turn itself into a fly, and with this it changes to the likeness of a fly, for it imagines that now it will be able to slip under the girl's arm and get at the man in bed. But it settles on a marrowbone which the girl was holding and crawls right into it, and the girl sticks a plug in the hole. Then she puts the bone in her pocket with the Sending inside it, and now she wakes the man.

He woke up at once, and was much amazed at being still alive. Then the girl asks him where the Sending is now, and he says he has no idea what has become of it. Then the girl says she had long suspected that those fellows out on the Isles were no great wizards. So now the man was very glad, and they both enjoyed Christmas and were quite contented.

But when New Year drew near, the man began to be silent, and the girl asks what the matter is. He says that the men of the Isles are now busy preparing another Sending, 'and they are all of them putting strength into it. It is to come here on New Year 's Eve, and there's nothing that can save me then.'

The girl said she would not cross that bridge before she came to it – 'and you ought not to be afraid of Sendings from those men in the Isles.'

She was as merry as could be, so lie felt ashamed of showing any weakness.

On New Year's Eve he says the Sending has come ashore – 'and it is advancing rapidly, for great strength has been put into it.'

The girl tells him to come out with her; he does so, and they walk till they come to a thicket. There she halts, and pulls some branches aside, and there in front of them is a slab of rock. The girl lifts the slab, and there underneath it is an underground chamber. They both go down into it, and a gloomy, ghastly place it is; there is one dim lamp, and it is burning human belly-fat in a human skull. In a bed near this lamp lies an old man, rather ghastly-looking; his eyes are blood-red, and all in all he is horrible enough for the man from the Isles to be quite impressed.

'Well, foster-daughter,' says the old man, 'there must be some-thing new going on if you are out and about. It's a long while since I saw you. What can I do for you now?'

Then the girl tells him everything that had happened to her, and all about the man, and about the first Sending. The old man asks her to let him see the bone. She does, and he seemed to turn into quite a different person as soon as he was holding it; he turned it round and round in all directions, and stroked it all over.

Then the girl says: 'Be quick and help me, foster-father, because my man is beginning to feel sleepy now, and that's a sign that the Sending will soon be here.'

The old man takes the plug out of the bone, and out comes the fly. He strokes and pats the fly, and says: 'Off you go now, and go to meet any Sendings from the Isles and swallow them up.'

Then there was a mighty crash, and the fly zoomed off, and it had grown so huge that one jaw touched the sky and the other scraped the ground; in this way it met all Sendings that came from the Isles, and so the man was saved.

So home they went from the underground chamber, the girl and the man from the Vestmanna Isles, and they settled on her farm. They got married soon after, and increased and multiplied and filled the land. And that's as much as I know about this story.

J.Á. I 321–3, from a schoolboy in Western Iceland, 1845. Sendings could appear in many forms, but that of a fly was extremely frequent (J.Á. I 334–8, 340, 374, 529, 591, 594, 596, 626). In north Norway too, in the seventeenth and eighteenth centuries, it was thought that magicians could send sickness in the form of a fly (Lid 1935, 35), and in other parts of Europe it was commonly believed that a witch's familiar might well be a fly. In Iceland, the correct method of dealing with a fly-Sending was to lure it into a bottle or bone, stop it up, and often wrap it in a magic bag made from a baby's or a foal's caul (J.Á. I 334–8, 374). Powerful magicians could safely release and redirect it, even against its original master, as the old man does here; usually, however, the container would be thrown into a bog or other remote spot, and anyone who found it would be wise to leave it alone (J.Á. I 320). The same method of exorcism of dangerous ghosts is often mentioned in English tales , where they are conjured down into a bottle, snuffbox, or occasionally a boot, which is generally thrown into water. Examples are given in Theo Brown, *The Fate of the Dead* (Ipswich and Cambridge, 1979), 24–34, 61, and in Jacqueline Simpson, 'Confrontational Ghost-Laying in England and Denmark' in *Northern Lights*, ed. Séamas Ó Catháin (Dublin, 2001), 305–15.

Unwonted sleepiness as a sign of the approach of a hostile supernatural being is already found in the sagas, in connection with *fylgjur*, 'accompanying spirits' (e.g. *Njáls saga* chapter 12, *Finnboga saga* chapters 39–40, fiorsteins fláttr uxafóts). Human fat burning in a skull-pan, or a fatty human rib used as a torch, were thought to give an unfailing light, but one that always burnt dim (J.Á. I 442–3).

THE PRIEST AND THE FARMER

There was once a certain priest who was an ill-tempered bully towards his parishioners. There was one farmer in the parish who had never given way to the priest, and harsh words had often passed between them, and the priest had always got the worst of it. The farmer was getting rather old at the time when this story took place.

It happened once that the farmer was out and about during the night, and had occasion to go past the priest's homestead. There he sees that the priest is grappling with a ghost in the churchyard, and can barely hold his own. He had raised quite a young girl who had died a little while before, yet she was so fierce that he could hardly stand up to her. The farmer watches the fun for a while, and then says: 'Bite her on the left nipple, man!' – and so he goes on his way. The priest takes the lesson to heart, after which he manages to overcome the lass. He then sends this ghost against the farmer, telling it to do its worst against him.

But the farmer faces the ghost and gets it inside the leg-bone of a horse; then he drives a plug into the bone and ties it up in a foal's caul, and lays it in the bottom of his chest. And so, many years go by in which nothing happens worth speaking of, and the farmer never takes the bone out again, and so it bothers nobody.

There comes a time when this farmer takes to his bed, having caught a sickness which he thinks will be his death. He had only one child, a daughter, who was his heir. The farmer calls for her and tells her about the horse-bone, where it is, and what is kept in it; he warns her not to take the plug out or disturb the bone in any way until twenty years after his death, but says that after that time there would hardly be any harm left in the ghost. And when the farmer has made all the arrangements he thinks necessary, he dies, and is given a most splendid funeral.

His daughter takes on the running of the farm after him, and marries, and goes on living on the same land where her father had lived. But her husband owned another piece of land far larger and better than this, and they both wanted to get hold of it by hook or by crook, even though it was not available for their use, because certain men had been living on it for many years.

It then occurs to them that it would be a good plan to take the plug out of the horse-bone and send whatever lives inside the bone against the farmers on that other piece of land, and so this they do. But once the ghost is out of the bone, it refuses to go, for it says it was sent to this very farm and nowhere else, and it will not go away until it has carried out its errand. The farmer and his wife stood there helpless; they knew no way to get rid of the ghost, and the upshot of the affair was that it remained with them and their descendants ever afterwards.

J.Á. I 334–5, from Jón Sigur>sson, Member of the Alflingi (d.1889). This necromantic priest is ludicrously inefficient, for a young girl who had been only a short while dead should be the easiest type of ghost to control (see p.165 above). For a variant of this tale, see J.Á. I 374–5, and for another cautionary tale on the perils of unplugging horse-bones, J.Á. I 335–6.

How Petur Got a Wall-Eye

There was a man living in Arskogsstrond whose name was Petur Jonsson; he died in 1829, at the age of eighty-five. He only had the sight of one eye, and the other was completely opaque; he had become wall-eyed like that early in his life, and the reason was, or so people said, that he had tried to learn black magic. For as soon as he thought he had mastered the art, he wanted to prove his power and raise the dead. In the middle of the night he went out to the churchyard at Greater Arskog, to set to work and do this feat. Everybody at the farm attached to the church was asleep, and the whole place was quiet.

Now Petur sets to, and does everything the rules say, and after long-drawn-out spells, a dead body begins to rise up. Petur thinks it a rather unpleasant-looking ghost, and his nerve fails him at the thought of licking its face – for it so happened, most unluckily, that it was his own mother he had waked. The old woman gets her strength back remarkably rapidly, lumbers to her feet, and attacks her son unmercifully. Each catches hold of the other in a wrestler's grip, and the longer they play this game, the more furious she gets.

Now, as for the priest who lived in the farmstead, he woke up in his bed in the course of the night, and being a man gifted with the second sight, knew that something was going on in the churchyard. He dresses quickly, comes out, and sees the wrestling match between Petur and the old woman – and things had come to such a pass that Petur was quite worn out. As soon as the old woman sees the priest, she spits into her son's eye, lets go of him, and disappears. And it is from this old woman's spit that Petur is said to have got his wall-eye.

J.Á. I 335 (*Draugur setur vagl á auga*), from a story current in Eyjafjör>ur. See Jón Hnefill A>alsteinsson, 'Wrestling with a Ghost in Icelandic Popular Belief', *Arv* 43 (1988), 7–20.

THE BLACK DEATH

When the Black Death was raging in Iceland, it never reached the West Fjords, because twelve wizards from the west country combined forces and all made a Sending to go out against it, and they put strength into this Sending.

Now the Black Death was sweeping across the country in the form of a vapour, which reached half way up the mountain slopes, and out as far as the fishing banks; this vapour was being guided by an old man who strode along the mountains, and an old woman who strode along the shore. The pair of them lodged one night with a tenant farmer on Svalbardsstrond; this man thought they seemed rather suspicious-looking, and so he stayed awake that night, though he pretended to be sleeping, and he heard them planning how to arrange their journey next day in order to lay waste the whole district. By morning, they had disappeared. The farmer was troubled, and went to find Helga of Grund, who owned the land, and told her what he had observed. She decided that the thing to do was to remove herself and all her household high up into the mountains, and the plan worked, as is well known.

When the vapour and the death-toll began moving westwards, the wizards had the Sending ready; it was a great bull flayed to the knees, and it dragged its flayed hide behind it. It met the old man and woman on the beach at the foot of the Gilsfjord Cliffs, where their paths were bound to converge; men with the second sight saw their encounter, and the end of it was that the bull caught them both in its hide, forced them down under it, and crushed them to pieces.

J.Á. I 347–8, from the Revd Skúli Gíslason (d.1888). The Black Death reached Iceland in 1402 and raged for two years, but it is not so common a theme for legends there as in the rest of Scandinavia (ML 7080, 7090; cf.

von Sydow 1931,136, 157,173–4; Christiansen 1964, 8–11). These latter also often personify the plague as a hideous old woman, travelling through the countryside with broom or rake; some tell how this personified plague was outwitted, others deal with the plight of solitary survivors (cf. 'The Wizards of the Vestmanna Isles'). For Sendings as flayed bulls, see the note to the following story. The blue vapour has a parallel in a Scottish tale, where the plague is described as 'slowly flying along the ground . . . in the shape of a little yellow cloud' (see Briggs, 1971, II 377).

See T.R. Tangherlini, 'Ships, Fogs, and Travelling Pairs: Plague Legend Migration in Scandinavia', *Journal of American Folklore* 400 (1988), 176–206; Terry Gunnell, 'Mists, Magicians and Murderous Children: International Migratory Legends Concerning the "Black Death" in Iceland', *Northern Lights* (ed. Seámas Ó Catháin, Dublin, 2001), 47–59.

THORGEIR'S BULL

There was a man called Thorgeir whom many called Thorgeir the Wizard; his brother was called Stefan, and nicknamed the Reciter, as he recited and sang amazingly well, and their father's name was Jon. A third man, named Andres, is also mentioned, who was an uncle of these two brothers; they all came from Fnjoskadal, and their fishing grounds lay off Hrisey Isle in Eyjafjord. These men are all said to have shared in the work when they made the Bull.

It is said that Thorgeir got a new-born calf from a woman on Hrisey Isle, slaughtered it where he thought best, flayed it from head to croup (some say from croup to tail) so that it would trail the whole skin behind it, and then put strength in it by magic. Yet even so the three kinsmen did not think they had done enough; they put in its bones the essence of eight creatures – the air, a bird, a man, a dog, a cat, a mouse, and two sorts of sea-beasts – so that there were nine natures in the Bull, including its cattle-nature. Because of this it could move equally easily in the air, on land or in the sea, and appear to one's eyes in any of the forms fitting the essences in it, just as it liked best. Though the Bull had been made in the way described, Thorgeir still thought there was a chance that it might be defeated, so he got a baby's caul, which gives victory, and draped it over it. As Thorgeir had done most towards preparing this Bull and putting strength in it, it was named after him and known as Thorgeir's Bull.

It so happened that Thorgeir had asked the hand of a woman named Gudrun Bessadottir, but she had refused him. They sent the Bull against her. For some time, however, the Bull could not overcome her; but in the end things got to such a pitch that she could find no peace anywhere because of him, and when she had to go from one farm to another, sometimes six or eight men would have to escort her, since few people thought themselves safe in her company. Even so, she would sometimes be snatched from the back of her horse and flung some fifteen or twenty feet away, even though so many were escorting her; but on the other hand, he would leave her in peace now and then. In the end, she met her death from the harm the Bull did her.

Once, Gudrun was attending a service in church; the Bull was tormenting her in church so that she had no peace, and she had such cruel shooting pains that she was lying helpless. So a man went outside the church, and he saw the Bull lying on the sloping roof of a house; one side of this house faced the church, and on the side which faced the other way lay the Bull, and he had laid his muzzle on the crest of the roof, so that the man could see right down into his open nostrils. It seemed to him that a grey string came from the Bull's nostrils and stretched right to the church. But by the time the man got far enough to see round to the other side of the house, the Bull's body was just disappearing.

A farmer named Magnus lived on the farm called Sund in Hofdahverfi; his wife was named Helga, and she was a near relation of Gudrun's. After Gudrun's death, the Bull mostly turned its attentions to Helga, and tormented her unceasingly. Up in Eyjafjord there was a man named Torfi who knew magic lore; his home was at Klukur. Torfi was asked to destroy the Bull and set Helga free. He came to Sund, and saw where the Bull had taken up his position; he was lying in the main room, right on top of Helga, and she complained a great deal about a weight pressing down on her, especially on her feet, although they were bare – and in fact, the Bull was lying just on top of them. Torfi did not manage to destroy the Bull, because he said he did not know whether the caul had been pulled off the child or been slit open at the feet and slipped off him in that way, for sometimes the one was done and sometimes the other, but while the Bull had the caul on it would be hard to defeat him. The story goes that Helga later met her death by the Bull's doing, and that he haunted the people of her house for a long while after.

Though Thorgeir's original intention for the Bull was to make him destroy Gudrun, he used him for playing tricks on various other people he thought he had a grudge against, for the Bull was always devoted to him, though he could be troublesome enough at times. Thorgeir would often send him to mount other men's cows and make them stampede, and scatter them far and wide. Sometimes, too, men heard him bellowing in fog or darkness.

On one occasion Thorgeir had come to Helgilsstadir for a prayer-meeting, but went outside several times before the meeting. When the meeting was about to start, the master of the house went outside with Thorgeir, and they saw something like a fog-bank over the mountain to the north, though elsewhere the weather was clear and bright. Then Thorgeir said: 'Devil take it, he'll get no further for the moment!' People thought that he meant the Bull, and was making use of the fact that one of its natures was that of air. But not long afterwards, a howling squall sprang up, and men thought the Bull had known of this beforehand; people often noticed similar things before storms and other untoward happenings.

There are tales current in the North Quarter that two ghosts, Lalli of Husavik and Skotta of Eyjafjord, joined forces against Thorgeir's Bull and drove him all the way up Fnjoskadal like a sledge-horse –

but the sledge that Lalli and Skotta were sitting on was the Bull's own hide, and the Bull was dragging the whole load by his tail.

Whenever the Bull could not successfully carry out some errand he had to do for Thorgeir, he would go home and attack Thorgeir himself, playing various tricks on him and trying to destroy him. And even though Thorgeir was very expert in wizardry, time and again it was extremely difficult for him to defend himself against the Bull, and he had to use all he knew if the Bull turned surly on him. One day the Bull made such a determined effort to kill Thorgeir that he, being at a loss what to do, turned and ran indoors to his wife. His wife was holding a young child of theirs, and in this crisis Thorgeir wanted to take the child and give it to the Bull to calm him, but his wife begged him with all her heart not to, but to take a heifer which they had in their cattle-shed and give her to him. Thorgeir did this; he loosed the heifer and drove her out. But when some time had passed, the heifer was found not far from the farmhouse, all ripped into little pieces.

It is not said that the Bull did any great harm after this, except that he often drove cows mad. Also, he used to follow Thorgeir's kinsmen, and Thorgeir feared him so much that he made his daughters (who were both called Ingibjorg) carry runic charms in their aprons to protect them from the Bull.

The Bull would take on different shapes when he appeared, as has been said – sometimes the likeness of a man or a dog, but most often that of a horned Bull, flayed as far as the tail, and dragging his bloody hide behind him by the tail. But whatever the shape he appeared in, he looked ugly enough, and most people feared him.

Thorgeir did not destroy the Bull before he died, or so most men say; indeed, there is a tale that when Thorgeir was on his death-bed and was at the point of death, a grey cat (or, some say, a black puppy) was seen lying crouched on his chest, and that that was one form of the Bull.

Some say this Bull was made at the beginning of the eighteenth century, and others towards the middle of that century. Thorgeir died in 1803, aged eighty-six.

J.Á. I 350–2, from Bjarni Jóhannsson and Gísli Kronra>sson. A variant account by another informant (J.Á. I 348–50) adds further details – that the bull was made from a flayed calf's head, an ox's hoof, and a dog's paw; that it could also appear as a dog or cat, or, on one occasion, as a grey horse with its back broken and its belly scraping the ground, with bloody wounds where its ears and tail were cut off. For a vision of a flayed calf raised by magic, see J.Á. I 553. There are similar flayed cattle with trailing hides in Swabian and Bavarian lore (Maurer, 78); there is also a skinless Scottish monster, the Nuckelavee, part man and part horse, with raw flesh exposed and thick black blood pulsating in its naked veins, which rises from the sea to blight crops, bring disease, and drive cattle mad with fear (Briggs 1967, 58). English ghosts too may appear as fearsome shape-shifting bulls, as in the legends of the Great Giant of Hennlys and of the Roaring Bull of Bagbury (Briggs 1971, I 487, 560–1); one at Millichope was flayed (C. Burne, *Shropshire Folklore*, 1883, p.642).

Torfi Sveinsson of Klúkur, who died in 1843 at the age of eighty-two, was famous as a seer and thief-finder, and for spells to relieve those oppressed by hauntings. Though widely reputed to be a magician, he never claimed such powers himself but 'would leave people to think as they pleased about it'; he was also believed to have a 'Speaking Spirit' at his command, for which see pp.189–90 (J.Á. I 435, 484–5; for two stories about him from Ólafur Davi>sson's collection, see Craigie 363–6).

LAPPISH BREECHES

People who wanted to gather money that would never fail them used to get themselves breeches called Old Nick's Breeches, or sometimes also Lappish Breeches (as Lapps are famous wizards), or Money Breeches, Corpse Breeches, or Papey Breeches (because the men on Papey Isle used to be so rich that it was thought uncanny).

A man who wants to have such breeches must make an agreement with someone still alive that as soon as the latter dies, he can have the use of his skin. As soon as this happens, the survivor goes to the churchyard by night and digs the dead man up. He then flays the skin off him from the waist down and slips it off in one piece, for he must take care that there is no hole in the breeches. He must put them on straight away, and they will grow to his flesh until he himself removes them in order to give them to someone else. But before the breeches can be of any use, he must first steal a coin from some wretchedly poor widow, at the moment between the reading of the Epistle and the Gospel on one of the three major church festivals of the year (or else, some say, on the next day after he puts them on), and put this coin in the pocket of them. After this, the breeches will draw money from living men, so that the pocket is never empty whenever their owner puts his hand in it; but he must take care never to take the stolen coin out.

A point worth noting about Lappish Breeches is that a man who has them cannot take them off or get rid of them just when he likes, but on the other hand the whole salvation of his soul depends on his doing so before he dies – not to mention the fact that his corpse will be all swarming with lice if he dies still wearing them. His one chance is to find someone who will step into them as he takes them off, and even so the only way he can do it is to step out of the right leg only at first, and for the man who has accepted them to step into it at once. As soon as he has done this, the new owner cannot change his mind even if he wants to, for if he tries to take his right leg out he will only find that he has put his left leg in without knowing how this happened. Then he in turn can never get rid of them except by the same method. Lappish Breeches keep their powers as they pass from man to man, and they never get torn.

J.Á. I 428–9, from stories current all over Iceland. Mensalder the Rich, who lived on Papey and died in 1799, was believed by his contemporaries to have owned such breeches and to have vanished at sea in a sudden squall because he could not bear to part with them (J.Á. I 429). It was also held that shoes of human skin would never wear out unless one trod on

consecrated ground in them (J.Á. I 443–4); magic gloves of human skin
are also mentioned (J.Á. I 543); for the Witch's Bridle, see pp. 194–5.

Similar ideas about the possible evil use of a corpse's skin may once
have been known in England. There is a legend recorded from two different parts of Devonshire of a wicked squire who sold not his soul but his
skin (posthumously) to the Devil; when the Devil tried to flay the corpse,
he found the skin full of holes, and hence useless to him (*Notes and
Queries* Series I, vol. III, 1851, 404; Tickler, *Dartmoor and its Borders*, 2nd
edition 1871, 117–18; cf. Briggs 1971, I 56, 153). In a Norwegian tale
(Christiansen 1964, 162–4), the Devil flays a corpse and wants to carry off
the skin to prove that the dead man belonged to him; a boy tricks him out
of the skin on the plea that he wants to make shoes of it.

In the present instance, the skin breeches function like various other
magical objects in European tradition which supposedly ensured a small
but perpetually renewed supply of money – e.g. the inexhaustible purse,
the brood penny, the mandrake laid in a money-box, and so forth. They
are gifts from the Devil, and if the owner cannot rid himself of them
before death, he is damned (Ward, 1981, I 93–8, 344–6).

THE TIDE MOUSE

There is another trick for getting wealth which will never fail,
which needs less magic, though still some, and this is to have a
Tide Mouse. This is how it is obtained. First, a man takes some hair
from a pure maiden, and with it he weaves a net with meshes
narrow enough to catch a mouse, this net must be laid in the sea
over some spot where he knows there is treasure lying on the sea-
bottom, for a Tide Mouse can only be found where there is silver
or gold. The net need not lie for more than one night if the spot is
well chosen, and the mouse will be in it by morning.

So now the man takes the mouse and brings it home and puts it
wherever he means to keep it. Some say it must be kept in a barrel

of wheat, others in a box; it must be given wheat to eat, and must lie on maiden's hair. One must take good care that it never slips out, for it always wants to get back to the sea. Next, one must steal a coin and lay it among the hair under the mouse, and the mouse then draws money out of the sea – every day one coin of the same value as that first laid under it, but this latter must never be taken out, or it will never draw money out again.

A man who has a Tide Mouse must take care to get rid of it before he dies, either by giving it to someone else or putting it in the sea, or else he will suffer great agony, and the mouse will go back to the sea of its own accord when the man dies, and this will cause terrible storms at sea. Everyone out at sea will be in dire peril, and there will be wild storms on land too, strong enough to turn everything topsy-turvy; these storms are thought the most dangerous storms of all, and are known as Mouse Squalls.

J.Á. I 429–30, from stories current in the south and west of Iceland. It has been suggested that the word *flæ>armús*, 'Mouse of the High Tide', is only a corruption or misunderstanding of the German *Fledermaus*, 'bat'. However, it does have some Scandinavian parallels, at least as regards its mode of action: e.g. the Swedish *spiritus*, a kind of magic insect which a man may buy and keep in a pouch, and which will every day draw to its owner as much money as he paid to get it, though to the risk of his soul if he does not rid himself of it before he dies (von Sydow 1931, 133). Moreover, the chief use of the mandrake root in Iceland was to draw buried silver out of the earth day by day (J.Á. I 645). Mice are common witches' familiars in Britain.

Jón Árnason mentions some exceptional storms which were believed to have been 'Mouse Squalls'; one was at the death of Bjarni Jónsson, a reputed wizard, in 1790, while another in January 1799 was held to be due to a Tide Mouse escaping from its owner, Jón of Fossi, and returning to the sea (J.Á. I 430).

THE CARRIER

If people want to grow rich by stealing milk or wool, they have discovered a handy way, which is to have a 'Carrier' or 'Spindle'. These are two names for the same thing, the former being current in the north of Iceland and the latter in the south and west, while in the east both are used; the former comes from its function, the latter from how it is prepared.

To get a Carrier, a woman must steal a dead man's rib from the churchyard on Whitsun morning, soon after he has been buried; then she wraps it in grey wool or yarn which she has stolen else-where (or others say she must pluck tufts from between the shoulders of a widow's sheep which has just had its wool plucked), wrapping it round the rib till it looks just like a twist of wool, and this she leaves lying between her breasts for a while. After this, she goes three times to Communion, and each time she lets the wine (or, some say, both bread and wine) dribble onto the materials which will form the Carrier, by spitting it into her bosom. Some say it need touch only one end of the Carrier, but most say both. The first time the woman dribbles on the Carrier, it lies quite still; the second time, it stirs; the third time, it is so strong and lively that it tries to jump out of her bosom. She must then be extremely careful that it should not be seen; if women were denounced as having Carriers, it is said that their punishment used to be to be burnt or drowned with the Carrier on them, so wicked and terrible was this thought to be. Justice was not thought properly carried out unless the Carrier had been pursued till it took refuge under the woman's skirt; her petticoat was then either tied up or sewn up below the Carrier, and both of them destroyed like that.

When the Carrier has been given its full strength in the manner described, the woman can no longer bear to keep it at her breast, so then she draws blood from the inside of her thigh, which causes a fleshy growth there, and she lets it suck there. It lives there and feeds on the woman's blood whenever it is at home, and for this reason one can always recognise those who are 'a Carrier's mother' because they are lame and have blood-red warts like fleshy growths inside their thighs. However, it appears that women also kept them in empty kegs or barrels in their dairies, at any rate sometimes. As soon as the Carrier's mother bears a child and has milk in her breasts, it will try to get at her, and if it does manage to suck her breast her life is at stake, for it will suck her to death.

The reason for having Carriers was to make them suck other people's cows (or, some say, ewes) out in the pastures. Afterwards they come to their mother through the dairy window while she is churning – for she has so arranged that the churn is standing right by the window while it is in use. When the Carrier comes to the window, it calls out, saying 'Full belly, Mummy!' or 'Churn lid off, Mummy!' Then the woman takes the churn lid off, saying 'Sick it up, dear son!' or 'Spew in the churn, little rogue!', or 'Let it go, son!'. Then it sicks up all it has sucked into its mother's churn so that plenty of butter forms in it.

Butter that comes from a Carrier's spew is known as Carrier Butter; outwardly it looks like other butter, but if one makes the Sign of the Cross over it or marks it with an X or with the pattern ✭, called the Butter Knot, it all breaks up into little pieces and looks curdled and clotted, till there is nothing to be seen but little flakes, or it even melts into froth. For this reason it is thought wiser, if one is offered sound butter at table or in a market, to make one or other of these marks on it. It has also sometimes happened that Carriers did not know the limits of their own stomachs, and so sucked more milk than they could carry home to their mother at the dairy window, in which case they vomit it up on the way home. People have often thought that they saw this 'Carriers' Spew' on the moors at the same season as Iceland Moss; it looks yellowish white, and thick.

When the Carrier sucks milk, it sets about it by jumping on the cow's back and coiling over her croup, and then making itself so long that it can reach the dugs from both sides at once, and it sucks through both its ends at once. But people who say that a Carrier has only one mouth say that it twists round on the croup as soon as it has sucked the dugs dry on one side, and then takes from the other side. It often happens that milch cows and ewes have a disease of the udders in which these swell and harden and the dugs become useless, and sometimes they never thrive again and have to be slaughtered. This udder disease is an inflammation, but people used to believe that it was due to milk being sucked by Carriers. To protect beasts against this disease, it was still the custom in some places in the nineteenth century to make the Sign of the Cross under the udder and over the croup, and to lay a Psalter on the spine.

Carriers had other uses besides sucking milch cows, for they could be used also for stealing wool, though this is more rarely mentioned. One spring day all the wool of a certain farm was being washed; the weather was good for drying, and all the wool was spread out in great swathes on the homefield. In the evening the weather looked set to be fine and dry again, so the wool was not even gathered into a heap, let alone taken indoors. When the people got up next morning, the wool seemed to have been all scraped into a heap, and when they went out to have a closer look, the first thing they knew was that they saw the whole mass whirl itself into a single huge skein, and thereupon the whole pile set itself in motion, except for a few scattered wisps – and those wisps were all the farmer got, for the big ball of wool rolled off so fast that there was no chance to follow it, and so vanished; and people believed that a Carrier must have wrapped the wool round itself and gone off with it.

When a Carrier's mother grows old and worn out, the Carrier troubles her so much that she can no longer bear to have him suck the nipple on her thigh. Then she sends him up into the mountains and orders him to gather up all the lambs' droppings from three pasture-lands, and he works himself to death over this, for he will do all he can to bring them all home to his mother, and never let himself rest. In proof of which, men have said that one often finds human ribs among heaps of lambs' droppings up on the pastures. Carriers are amazingly rapid, and go hurtling over hill and dale; sometimes they seem to roll like a clew of thread or a skein of wool, or sometimes they leap along on one end. There are a few examples of men who chased them on horseback, but only on the swiftest of horses. When pursued, a Carrier will hide himself under his mother's skirts, and so the man who sees this can tie her clothes around her legs and have her put to death.

J.Á. I 430–3. For anecdotes illustrating various points, particularly tales of men who saw a Carrier at work and chased it till it took refuge beneath its owner's skirts, see J.Á. I 433–5. The term *tilberi*, 'carrier', is used in the north of Iceland, and *snakkur*, probably meaning 'spindle wrapped in yarn', in the south and west; in the east both terms are used. The tale of the Carrier making off with the wool is from the East Quarter. Belief in the Carrier cannot be traced back any earlier than the seventeenth century in Iceland, though one writer of that period claims that a woman was burnt in 1500 for having one (Sveinsson 1940, 177).

In Sweden and Finland there are closely similar ideas about the *bjära*, 'carrier', also known as 'milk-hare' or 'troll-cat'. It can be made out of various objects, such as a stick burnt at both ends, a spindle wrapped in wool, or a stocking-leg; it is brought to life by three drops of the woman's blood, or of stolen milk, and is sent to suck milk and spew it up, as in Iceland. It may take the form of an animal, especially a hare or cat, in which case, if it is shot, milk will spurt from it (Craigie 337; von Sydow 1931, 132–3; von Sydow in Lid 1935, 125–6; Kvideland and Sehmsdorf, 175–7). In the Icelandic tradition, the choice of a human rib should presumably be seen as a blasphemous parody of God's creation of Eve (from one of Adam's ribs). In Denmark, however, as in the rest of Europe generally, it is thought that the witch herself takes on the form of a hare or sends out her soul in this form. For an unusual English tale, in which the witch's emissary, though appearing as a goose, was in fact a magically animated jug, see Briggs 1971, I 56, 153.

THE SPEAKING SPIRIT

If a man wants to know the future, all he need do is to procure himself a Speaking Spirit, and this will tell him all he wants to know. In this it resembles the spirits or ghosts that appear to some men in dreams to give them information or warnings, but a Speaking Spirit talks to one when one is awake, and one needs far more magic to get oneself a Speaking Spirit than a Dream Man.

If a man wants to obtain a Speaking Spirit, he must first go off quite alone to some spot where he knows that no one will come, for his life will be forfeit if he is interrupted while he is calling the spirit to him by magic chants. He must lie down in the shade and turn towards the north. He must stretch a foal's caul over his mouth and nose, and then read aloud certain magic rhymes. The caul is sucked into his mouth as he chants, and then the spirit comes and tries to get down inside the man, but the caul blocks the way, and as soon as it is there, the man clenches his teeth together. So then the spirit is trapped inside the caul, and the man puts the caul in a box, with the spirit inside it.

The spirit will not speak until the man has sprinkled it with Communion wine; to do this, he must have the box with the spirit inside it under his neckerchief when he goes to Communion, and then spit the wine into it. One can also give a Speaking Spirit maydew, but this is not essential. The Speaking Spirit tells its owner everything he wants to know, but it is most willing to talk during heavy storms or on nights when the wind is in the east. If it slips out of the box, it will enter into its owner and drive him mad.

A certain Torfi, who lived at Klukur in Eyjafjord, had a Speaking Spirit which had grown hoarse with old age and neglect; it used to declare that it had come down from the thirteenth century, passing from one man to another. I have never heard tell who it had been in its lifetime – for a Speaking Spirit is the wraith of a dead man. When a man is fey, his Speaking Spirit will begin to lie to him, but not before.

Torfi passed on his Speaking Spirit to a certain Sigfus of Efstaland in Oxnadal, and when he in turn was old he wanted to pass it on to Jon of Audnir in Oxnadal, but he would not take it. This spirit was kept in a red oak box. When Sigfus felt he had not long to live, he went out to Engimyra Knoll one night, and took Jon with him. They buried the box in the knoll, and Sigfus prepared its grave and blessed it. Jon asked him why he blessed the spirit's grave, and Sigfus said: 'I'm blessing it in the Devil's name, my friend.'

Some people think they have seen a wraith above this spirit's grave, and in the 1860s people still remembered where it lies. There is a curse that follows Speaking Spirits, namely that wherever there is one buried on a farm, the man and wife there will never get on well together, and it is thought that this has proved to be the case on this farm.

J.Á. I 435–6. This belief was already current in the sixteenth century. According to other versions, the would-be seer might have to wait as long as three or even six days before the spirit would come; a calf's caul, a horsehide bag, or a simple cloth might be used, and the captured spirit should be kept in a horse's hoof (J.Á. I 130, Maurer 94). Torfi of Klúkur is the same man as was mentioned above as failing to exorcise Thorgeir's Bull; Sigfús fiorleifsson, to whom he is here said to have given the spirit, died in 1829, but Torfi himself lived till 1843. The anecdote about them is from a schoolboy from northern Iceland in 1845. For the 'Dream Man', see the note to 'The Lovers' above, p. 123–4.

SITTING OUT AT CROSSROADS

The purpose of this rite is to call up the dead, not in order to send them against other people, but so as to question them; it is several times referred to in medieval texts, but it has left few traces in later oral tradition, where 'sitting out' is associated with the belief in elves more than with that in the dead. The rite must be carried out on New Year's Eve or on the Eve of St John's Day (24 June); the former date is the more general, and applies to the belief in both ghosts and elves.

He who wants to learn things by 'sitting out' must make his preparations to go out on New Year's Eve, taking with him a grey cat, a grey sheepskin with its fleece on, the hide of a walrus or (others say) of an old bull, and an axe. Taking all these with him, the magician must go to a crossroads where four roads run, each in a straight unbroken line, to four churches. He must lie down in the crossroads itself, spread the hide over him, and tuck it in well on every side, so that no part of his body sticks out from underneath it. He must hold the axe in his hands and stare fixedly at the edge of it, and never look either to right or to left whatever may appear to him, nor ever answer a single word if he is spoken to. In this position he must lie, still as a corpse, till day breaks next morning.

As soon as the magician had arranged himself, he would begin reciting the formulas and spells that served to call up the dead. At this, if he had any relations buried in one or more of the four churches to which the roads led, they would come to him and tell him all he wished to know about past and future happenings through many generations. If he had the firmness of mind to face the edge of the axe and never take his eyes off it or let one word pass his lips, whatever happened, he could not only remember all that the dead had told him but could also go again in safety whenever he wished, so as to question them about anything he desired to know by 'sitting out'. But people cannot remember anybody who returned from sitting at the crossroads without suffering for it in some way.

J.Á. I 436–7. Cf. the practice described above, pp.70–2, for summoning elves at crossroads. This form of necromancy can be traced back to heathen times in the Icelandic Eddic poems *Hávamál* and *Vǫluspá*, and also in Norway, where men seeking occult wisdom would 'sit out' on burial-mounds (*Hallfre>ar saga* chapter 6), and where Christian laws forbade men on pain of death to 'go on seers' journeys and sit out so as to raise trolls up, and thus do heathen magic' (Gulaflíngslǫg). In the ecclesiastical *Maríu saga*, thought to be by Kygri-Bjǫrn Hjaltason (d.1237–8), a would-be seer is advised to go to a lonely forest, lay a freshly flayed ox-hide on the ground, draw nine squares round it with devilish incantations, and then sit on it till the Devil comes to reveal the future. Whether by 'the Devil' Kygri-Bjǫrn meant a dead man, an elf, or a troll is unfortunately impossible to tell.

The same practice was known on the Faroes, where, as in Iceland, it was sometimes the dead and sometimes elves (there called 'trolls'), who came, bringing treasures and seeking to break the seer's concentration (see Craigie 383–4 for a version with trolls, and Williamson 234 for one with ghosts, taken from J. Jakobsen's *Faerösk Folkesagn og Aevintýr*, 1898–1901).

The instructions given here apparently contain a built-in impossibility. The Icelandic landscape is traversed by numerous rivers, ravines, and mountain ridges, and churches are few; it is extremely unlikely that there has ever been a crossroads 'where four roads run, each in a straight unbroken line, to four churches'. The instructions for seeing elves on the move (above, pp.70-2) are simpler; there, all the seer needs is a crossroads on the moors from which four churches can be seen.

ANIMAL PLAGUES

A man who wants to injure his enemies can either send them a Sending, which has been described already, or a *stefnivargr*, which literally means 'a wolf aimed at another', and refers to any animals that are given magic strength and then sent out against others to do them harm and injury.

There was once a rich man who lived out on the Akureyjar Isles, an absolute skinflint who always grudged giving any help to the poor. In revenge, a certain wizard sent him such a devastating host of mice that they destroyed everything he owned, and in the end he died in abject poverty. For a long time afterwards the mice remained on the islands, until a new landlord sent for another wizard. The latter arrived and gave orders for a whole leg of mutton to be roasted, and then sat down in the open air and settled down to eat it. All at once, the mice arrived in crowds and gathered round to get a bite of it. The wizard stood up, took the leg of mutton in his hand, and went back into the farmhouse and so through every room in it, and then out again and so all round the island, until every single mouse on the island had come out to him. Then he flung the leg into a deep pit, which he had earlier had dug in readiness. All the mice sprang into the pit after the meat; then he had the pit covered over at once, and strictly forbade anyone to disturb it from then on. After that there were no mice on the Akureyjar Isles for a long time. Many years later, the then owner ordered foundations for a new building to be laid at this spot, and his men were so careless as to reopen the pit. Then the mice rushed out again in a twinkling of an eye, and ever since, to this very day, they have been a plague on these islands which in other ways are such good land.

A certain Icelander once spent a winter in Finnmark, and an old woman on the farm where he stayed wanted to marry him, but he did not want her, and went home next spring. The old woman was mightily annoyed, and decided to avenge herself. She took two foxes, one male and one female, and chanted spells over them. Then she got the foxes on board a ship going to Iceland, and decreed that they were to increase and multiply there, so that the land would never be free of them; also, they were to attack the first kind of animal they would see in that land. Now the old woman thought the foxes would see men first, and intended that they should destroy them; but the ship they were on went aground in the East Quarter, and the foxes leapt ashore on the headland that ever since then has been called Melrakkanes, 'Foxes' Headland'. There they saw a flock of sheep, and these were the first kind of animal they saw in the country. They have since then increased and multiplied and spread all over the country, and they attack sheep and kill them.

J.Á. I 439 (*Stefnivargur*); the story of the mice is from Maurer 94–5, and that of the foxes from a schoolboy in Múlasýsla in 1845. The belief in a wizard's ability to drive or lure mice away, sometimes into a cave, was current already in the seventeenth century; it is mentioned in Bishop Gísli Oddsson's *De Mirabilibus Islandiæ*, 1637. Norwegian examples are classified by Christiansen under ML 3060, 'Banning the Snakes'; British ones under 3061★ 'The Pied Piper' (Briggs 1971, II 307–8). That a cruel miser should be punished by a plague of rats or mice was common in medieval European local legends; some examples, including that of Bishop Hatto, are given in S. Baring-Gould, *Curious Myths of the Middle Ages*, 1877, 447–56.

THE WITCH'S BRIDLE

Whoever wants to be able to ride through the air and across water must have the Witch-Ride Bridle. To make this, one should dig up a newly buried corpse and tear a strip of skin off the whole length of the spine; this will be used as reins. Next, one must flay the dead man's scalp off and use it for the head-piece of the bridle; the hyoid bones are to be used as the bit and the hip bones as cheek-pieces. It is also necessary to chant spells over the bridle, and then the bridle is ready; nothing more is needed now but to lay the bridle on any man or beast, stock or stone, and then it will rise up into the air with whoever is sitting on it and will fly quicker than lightning wherever one wants to go. There is then a loud whistling sound in the air, and some men believe they have heard this, and even the rattling of the bridle itself.

J.Á. I 440 (*Gandrei>arbeizli*), from stories current in Borgarfjör>ur. The word I have here translated 'witch-ride', *gandrei>*, was of much wider application in thirteenth- and fourteenth-century sagas, where it is variously used of an ominous figure seen riding through the skies, of a she-troll riding by night to a gathering of trolls, and of an elf-boy riding a magic stick (*Njáls saga* chapter 12, *Ketils saga hœngs* chapter 5, and fiorsteins fláttr bœjarmagns). Other phrases using the word *gandr* (the precise meaning of which is unknown, though it always refers to magic) are applied to the shamanistic sending-out of the soul in sleep or trance, and to shape-changing (Lid 1935, 37–9).

None of these older passages mentions any bridle; the gruesome use of skin and bones is quite typical of the macabre procedures of seventeenth-century Icelandic magic. The effect of the bridle is illustrated in the story of 'Hild the Queen of the Elves' (pp. 57–65 above), and also in one about a servant-lad whose mistress rode on him to a Sabbath, where a coven of twelve women were studying black magic under Satan's tuition (J.Á. I 440–1, translated in Kvideland and Sehmsdorf, 185–7). This latter tale has strong Continental affiliations, and is not typical of Icelandic witchcraft beliefs, in which the ride and the Sabbath play a very minor role (Davi>sson 1940–3, 55). Witches' bridles are known in English lore too; there was mention of one in the second Lancashire witch trial in 1634, and it is also a feature of local legends of the type ML 3057*, 'The Witch-Ridden Boy' (Briggs 1962, 102–3, 253; 1971, II 623–4, 715, 749–50).

THOR'S HAMMER

If a man owns a 'Thor's Hammer', he will know who it is who has robbed him if he loses anything. To make this hammer, one must have copper from a church bell, three times stolen. The hammer must be hardened in human blood on a Whitsunday, between the reading of the Epistle and the Gospel. A spike must also be forged out of the same material as the hammer, and this spike one must jab against the head of the hammer, saying: 'I drive this in the eye of the Father of War, I drive this in the eye of the

Father of the Slain, I drive this in the eye of Thor of the Aesir.' The thief will then feel pain in his eyes; if he does not return the stolen goods, the procedure is repeated, and then the thief will lose one eye; but should it prove necessary to repeat it a third time, he will lose the other eye too.

Another method is for a man to steal a copper bell from a church between the Epistle and Gospel, and make a hammer from it. When he wants to know who the thief is, he must take a sheet of paper and draw a man's eyes on it, or, better still, a whole face with two eyes, using his own blood, and on the reverse of the sheet draw a suitable magic sign. Next, he must take a steel spike and set one end of it on the eye and strike the other end with the Thor's Hammer, saying 'I am giving eye-ache to the man who robbed me', or 'I am knocking out the eye of the man who robbed me.' Then the thief will lose one eye, or both, if he does not give himself up first.

J.Á. I 445, from a story current in Northern Iceland. An actual hammer of this type was seen by Maurer in 1858; it had been given to his informant's late husband many years before by an old woman reputed to be learned in magic; it was made of copper, about three inches long, with a detachable handle to be used as the jabbing spike. The idea of punishing a thief by magically knocking out his eye is common in the three other Scandinavian lands, both in learned books of magic and in popular practice; in the latter case, it is almost always a blacksmith who carries out the rite (von Sydow 1931, 133, 151; Lid 1935, 44–535). A smith, with his hammers and fiery forge, makes a very appropriate surrogate for fiórr. The 'suitable magic sign' mentioned in the text may possibly be one called 'Thor's Hammer' which resembles the swastika, the god's symbol in heathen times: ⌗ (J.Á. I 446). A Danish conjuration to be repeated while three times hammering a nail into a drawing of an eye is given in Kvideland and Sehmsdorf, 148–9.

6

BURIED TREASURE

THE TREASURE OF FAGRIHOLL

Not very far from Stykkisholur is a hillock called Fagriholl in which, so they say, all the riches of the old monastery at Helgafell lie buried. There was an attempt made once to dig into this hillock, and as soon as the diggers had got fairly deep into it, it seemed to them as if Helgafell Church was all ablaze, and they ran to put the fire out. Later, preparations were made to dig into it a second time, and this time they thought that armed men came up out of the ground and threatened to kill them if they did not stop digging. After this, no native Icelanders could be found willing to dig into this hillock, so some Danes were got for the work, but the attempt proved fruitless.

J.Á. I 279, from Maurer 72. Maurer's informant, Egill Sveinbjarnarson Egilsson, was the owner of the land on which this hillock stood, and it was he himself who had been forced by local hostility to hire Danes when he wished to open it up. Helgafell Monastery was sacked in the 1540s by men sent by the King of Denmark to impose the Reformation on Iceland; according to Jón Gumun>sson the Learned (d.1658), its manuscripts were burnt, and the parson guilty of this desecration died by drowning the following year, 'as a punishment'.

Tales such as this and the next one fall into the widespread group ML 8010, 'Buried Treasure', which has many local variations; frequently recurring motifs include eerie sights, illusions of fire, monstrous or ghostly guardians, a taboo on speaking, and last-minute catastrophes (for a few Danish examples, see Craigie 407–12; for a Norwegian one, Christiansen 1964, 23–4; for a summary of Swedish material, von Sydow 1931, 129–30). Further examples will be found in Lindow 76–7; Simpson 1988, 34–8;

Kvideland and Sehmsdorf, 321–4. In the similar English legends, it is often thunderstorms or phantom horses that scare away the treasure-seekers (Briggs 1971, II 337–8, 380), but illusions of fire occur too (Briggs 1971, II 213, 'The Gold of Craufurdland').

Jón Árnason put these tales into the section on ghosts, because in Iceland buried hoards are thought of as belonging to and guarded by the dead. There is a plain link with the ancient belief, the basis of many episodes in sagas, that dead men in their burial mounds keep guard over the wealth and fine weapons buried with them; but whereas in sagas the hero always defeats the dead man and carries off the treasures, in the later folktales the seekers are always baffled and the treasure lost. Similarly, in *Grettis saga* chapter 18 the hero successfully wins treasure, the existence of which he learnt from seeing blue flames flickering about a burial mound, but in later tales (J.Á. I 276–7) such flames vanish before they can be tracked down.

For other tales of treasures guarded by illusions, see J.Á. I 149, 276–80, 488; II 80, 84.

THE CHEST OF GOLD

A burial mound stands in Vatnsfjord Parish in the west country, near Isafjord. There is a chest of gold hidden in it which people have often tried to get at, but they have always had to stop on account of the horrible visions which appeared when the mound was dug up. Once, two enterprising young men agreed to go and break into this mound, and they dug until they saw the chest. It was so heavy that they could not lift it, though they were sturdy fellows, so they dug all round its sides, and underneath it too. The chest had very strong iron bands round it, with rings at each end. So now one of them got down under the chest and lifted it, while the other hauled on it by a rope tied to one of these rings. But as soon as the chest was raised, the ring broke away from the end, so that it crashed onto the man beneath, and he died at once. The man who was up above was frightened, abandoned the work, and fled, but kept the ring. It was a great big copper ring, and he gave it to Vatnsfjord Church, where it is on the church door to this day.

Other people say that certain men had agreed to dig the mound up. They found the chest, bound with iron, and with rings at each end of it. They passed a rope through the rings and pulled, but one man stayed down in the hole to lift the chest from below. By the time the chest was almost level with the brink, the men above were pretty near exhausted, and thought it more than doubtful whether it would come up or not.

Then one of them said: 'It will come up, if God wills.'

Then the one who was down below lifting the chest yells out: 'It *must* come up, whether God wills or not!'

At that, one of the end rings broke off, so that the chest fell on the man below and killed him, and the sides of the pit caved in. The others ran off, terrified, and gave the ring to Vatnsfjord Church, and stopped digging altogether.

J.Á. I 279, from a schoolboy in the west of Iceland in 1845. For another tale in which treasure seekers got only a broken ring-handle for their pains, and gave it to the local church, see J.Á. I 488. Two other churches are said to have as door-handles rings broken from a giantess' treasure-chest; for a different aetiological legend about a door-handle, see the story of Bergthor, pp.98–100 above. The second part of the present tale, with the motif of the man who would not say 'if God wills', is closely paralleled in a legend attached to the supposed grave-mound of Ingólfr Árnason, the first settler of Iceland (J.Á. II 75); it has very many international parallels in stories about buried treasures or sunken bells. (An English one, attached to Willy Howe in Yorkshire, is given in Briggs 1971, II 396.)

THE DREAMER AND THE TREASURE

A good many men were once travelling together, and one Sunday morning they pitched tent on a pleasant grassy field; the weather was clear and bright. These men all lay down to sleep, lying in a row in the tent. The one nearest the entrance could not get to sleep, so he was looking at one thing or another in the tent. Then he saw a wisp of bluish vapour hovering above the man who lay furthest in, and then this wisp drifted through the tent and out into the open.

The man wanted to know what this could be, so he followed the vapour. It drifted gently, very gently, across the field, and finally came to where an old horse-hide and skull were lying; these were full of blowflies, and they were buzzing loudly. The vapour drifted inside the horse skull. A good while later, it came out again and drifted off across the field once more, till it came to a tiny brook which ran through the field. It followed the course of this down-stream, and it looked to the man as if it was trying to cross. The man was carrying a whip, and this he laid right across the brook (for it was so narrow that the handle could reach right across), and the wisp of vapour went along the handle of the whip and so drifted across the brook. Then it went on again, and eventually reached a little tussock in the field. The vapour vanished down inside this. The man stood and waited for it to come back. Soon it came. Then it went back again along the same track as it had come; the man laid his whip across the brook and the vapour crossed along it as before, and then it went straight home to the tent, never stopping till it was hovering over the man who lay furthest in, and then it disappeared. Then the other man lay down and fell asleep.

Towards evening the travellers got up and fetched their horses, and as they were busy loading them up, they chatted of this and that, and among other things the man who had been sleeping at the inner end of the tent said: 'I wish I owned what I was dreaming of today.'

'What was it? What did you dream of?' says the one who had seen the vapour.

The other says: 'I thought I was walking about out here on this field. Then I came to a splendid large house where a crowd had gathered and were singing and playing with the greatest merriment and glee, and I stayed a long time in that house. When I came out again, I walked a long, long way across fine level plains, until I came to a broad river which I tried for a long time to cross, but I could not. Then I saw a terrifyingly huge giant coming; he was carrying an enormous big tree in his hand which he laid across the river, and so I crossed it by way of the tree.

Then I walked on again for a long, long way, till I came to a huge burial mound. It was open, and I went in, and what did I find there but a great barrel, full of money! I stayed an immensely long time in there, staring at the money, for I had never seen such a heap as that before. Then I came out again and went home by the same way as I had come, and when I reached the river the same giant came with his tree and laid it across, so that I crossed by way of the tree, and so came home again to the tent.'

The man who had tracked the vapour was filled with secret glee, and says to the one who had had this dream: 'Come along, my friend, let's both go and look for that money at once.'

The other burst out laughing, thinking that he wasn't quite right in the head, but all the same he did go. They follow the route which the vapour had taken, come to the tussock, and dig it up, and there they find a keg full of money. Then they went back to their companions, told them the whole story of the dream and vapour, and showed them the keg of treasure.

J.Á. I 356–7, from an old woman in Borgarfjör>ur. The Icelandic title of this tale, *Dalakúturinn*, 'The Keg of Treasure', shows that in the narrator's mind its chief interest lay in its ending, and I have therefore put it in this section. However, in essence it is, as Jón Árnason points out, related to ancient beliefs about the nature of the soul, and hence to tales of shape-shifting, and so does not come into any of the main categories of more recent Icelandic beliefs and tales. It is an example of ML 4000, 'The Soul of a Sleeper Wanders on its Own', sometimes also known as the 'Guntram

Legend' because it first occurs in the *History of the Longobards* by Paul the Deacon (d.790), where it is told of the soul of King Guntram of Burgundy (translated in Ward, II 58; the soul there is seen as a small animal like a snake, not as a vapour). See also Michael Chesnutt, 'Nordic Variants of the Guntram Legend', *Arv* 47 (1991), 153–65. The tale is widely known in Western Europe, occurs also in central Asia, and is common in Japan; for two Norwegian examples, see Christiansen 1964, 47–8. In its basic form there is no mention of treasure, but the few instances where this is included are also classified as AT 1645 A, 'A Dream of Treasure Bought'. For a close Scottish parallel recorded in 1852, see Briggs 1971, II 583–4.

The idea of a *féfl úfa*, 'money tussock', occurs in several tales, and was believed in many parts of Iceland; elves, mermen or ghosts may reveal its existence (J.Á. I 61, 132–4, 307–8). The present tale shows clearly its relationship to the old idea of treasures in a burial mound, the small tussock appearing a great burial mound to the dreamer.

7

GOD AND THE DEVIL

What Old Nick Got out of Man

No sooner had God set to work to create man, than the Devil was filled with malice and wanted to try to harm him. So Old Nick loops his tail up behind him, goes off to find Almighty God, and asks Him to give him the tips of man's longer fingers, these tips being all of different lengths, so that then all the fingers should be of equal length. God promised him that he could have the longer bits, provided that the fingers really are of different lengths once the hand is clenched. So anybody whose fingers are not all even when they touch his palm, had better beware of losing the top joint of his fingers.

When Old Nick saw he would never make much profit out of this promise of the Lord's, he asked the Lord to give him the muck which a man drops when he goes into the fields to ease himself. The Lord gave him permission to take it, provided the man does not look behind him when he has finished what he wanted to do. But most men do look behind them, so they say.

When Old Nick saw he would get nothing from this either, he asked God for the bits of finger-nail which men cut or clip off. God promised he could have them if the whole nail was trimmed in one piece and not broken up afterwards, but if it was cut in three sections, Old Nick would get none of them. Therefore all men cut their nails in three or more sections; for otherwise Old Nick stores up the trimmings, if they are cut off in one piece and not snapped in two afterwards, and he makes strips of shoe-leather out of them until he has some shoes to wear, and this does indeed happen from time to time.

J.Á. II 2–3 (*Snemma beygist krókurinn, sem ver>a vill*), from a story generally current in Northern Iceland. The taboo on trimming nails in one piece was widespread, and an alternative explanation offered was that the Devil would use such trimmings to build (or to nail together) a 'ship of the dead' (J.Á. II 549). This type of belief can be traced back to pagan myths; in Snorri Sturluson's *Edda* (*c.*1220) it is said that at the Doom of the Gods some of their demonic foes will come in *Naglfar*, a ship built from dead men's nails, and so a man who dies with untrimmed nails helps to hasten the building of that ship. Conversely, also according to Snorri, leather trimmings thrown away in shoe-making help the gods, for they go to make the shoe with which Ó>inn's son Ví>arr will trample on the great Wolf's jaw.

OLD HORNIE TRIED TO MAKE A MAN

The Devil wanted to be just as clever as God, so he set to work in the hope of creating a man. But his experiment did not turn out to be a great success, for instead of his making a man, the final result was a cat – and furthermore there was no skin on it.

Saint Peter took pity on the creature and made a skin for the cat, as the verse says:

> *Old Hornie tried to make a man,*
> *And got a cat without a skin;*
> *Saint Peter hit on a good plan –*
> *A fur to wrap the pussy in.*

Indeed, the cat's fur is the only part of the beast which is any good.

J.Á. II 3, a story current throughout Iceland. Other humorous tales also illustrate the Devil's inefficiency as a creator; he is said to have tried to put out the newly created sun by pissing at it, but only managed to form Lake Mývatn in the process (J.Á. II 2). There is a pun here on *mý* 'mosquito' and *míga* 'to piss'; moreover, the mosquitoes that infest this lake are said to have sprung to life from the vermin in the Devil's beard (J.Á. I 627).

THE HALIBUT, THE LUMPSUCKER, AND THE JELLYFISH

One day Jesus Christ was walking by the sea, and Saint Peter with him. Christ spat in the sea, and from this came the halibut. Then Saint Peter also spat in the sea, and from this came the lumpsucker; both fish are considered good eating, but all the same the halibut is the superior dish. The Devil came sneaking up behind them and saw what was going on; he wanted to be just as good as the others, so he too spat in the sea, but from his spittle came the jellyfish, which is no good at all.

J.Á. II 3, from a story current in Borgarfjör>ur. St Peter is here shown as a minor creator, well-intentioned, but less powerful than Christ; as in the previous tale, though he cannot equal God's achievements, he does easily surpass those of the Devil.

OLD NICK SPEAKS LATIN

Once, a priest who was a pretty ignorant fellow had to baptise a baby, in the days when it was the custom to drive the Devil out from the baby by an exorcism, and in Latin too.

So this priest says: 'Abi, male spirite!'

But Old Nick himself was sitting in a corner of the church, and at this he lets out a howl, and says: 'Pessime grammatice!'

Then the priest says: 'Abi, male spiritu!'

And Old Nick says: 'Ye lee'd afore, and lee the noo!'

Then the priest says: 'Abi, male spiritus!'

And at this Old Nick took himself off, remarking as he went: 'Sic debuisti dicere prius.'

J.Á. II 23, from the Revd Búi Jónsson (d. 1848). In a German parallel given by Maurer (106–7), the Devil wins; the dialogue runs thus: *Exi tu ex hoc corpo – Nolvo – Cur tu nolvis? – Quia tu male linguis – Hoc est aliud rem*, says the priest, and abandons the attempt. I am indebted to Benedikt Benedikz for pointing out that by giving Old Nick a Scots accent the literal sense of his retort and its rhyme can both be perfectly preserved.

THE GOBLIN ON THE CHURCH-BEAM

There was once a priest, though of which parish is not said, who was saying Mass one Sunday as usual, and everything was going along quite correctly as it normally did; nothing odd happened until he had gone up into the pulpit and begun preaching his sermon, but then a man at the front of the church burst out laughing in the course of the sermon. Nobody showed that they had noticed at the time, neither the priest nor anyone else, and indeed it only happened the once. So the priest completed his sermon, returned to the altar, and went on with the Mass to the end.

As soon as it was over, the priest inquired who the man had been who had so scandalised the congregation, and he was told who it was. Then the priest sent for this man and asked him what he had found so funny in what he had been saying from the pulpit that day that he could not restrain his laughter, and so had scandalised the congregation; or if not, what else had made him act in that way.

The man said it would never enter his head to laugh at the priest's teaching – 'but I saw something which you probably did not see, Father,' says he, 'nor anyone else in the congregation, very likely.'

'What was that?' says the priest.

'When you had just gone up into the pulpit, Father, two old women sitting in the corner pew on the women's side at the back of the church began to tear each other to pieces, each hurling unforgivable insults at the other. At that moment I happened to look up at the cross-beam, and I saw that a goblin had appeared up there. In one paw he clutched a shrivelled leather boot, and in the other he held a horse's leg-bone. This goblin was poking out his little skull-cap to catch every filthy word the old women let fly, and frantically writing down everything they said on this patched-up boot, writing with the horse-bone, while they went on and on and on.

'There came a time when there was no more room on the boot; so this devil, not at all at a loss, sets to work and stretches it, holding one end in his fangs and the other in his claws, and so he makes it last a while longer. Then on he goes again with furious energy, until the whole boot is scribbled over; then he does as before, stretches the boot, and so gets back to his writing. So it goes on, time after time; the goblin stretches the boot this way and that way, whenever there is no more room left on it.

'In the end, though, there comes a time when he has covered the boot with writing right up to the eyelets, and has stretched it out so thin that there's no stretch left in it; but since the old women are still going it hammer and tongs, and the goblin can't bear to miss a single one of their filthy words, he sets to work once more and stretches it with all his strength. And just as he's got his teeth well and truly into it, the boot splits, and at that the goblin topples back-wards off the cross-beam, and he would have landed smack on his bum on the church floor if it wasn't that just as he's on his way, just tumbling down, he drives his claws hard into the beam. And then, Father, I couldn't help laughing – and I humbly beg your pardon, and that of the congregation, if I caused scandal.'

The priest decided that the man could be excused for what had happened, and set him a light penance only, as an example to others; but he said the old women ought to have something better to do in church than to keep the devils amused with their disgraceful language.

J.Á. II 4–5, from Sigur>ur Gu>mundsson (d.1874). This amusing *exemplum*, first found in the collection by Jacques de Vitry, was already known in Iceland in the thirteenth century, for it occurs in *Maríu saga*, an ecclesiastical work probably by Kygri-Bjǫrn Hjaltason (d.1237 or 1238) (ed. C.R. Unger, pp.176-7). It is classified as AT 826 'The Devil writes Down Names of Men on Hide in Church', and is popular as a folktale in Germany, Lithuania, and Sweden, occurring also in other Baltic and Slavonic areas. (Cf. F.C, Tubach, *Index Exemplorum*, number 1630; R. Wildhaber, *Das Sündenregister auf der Kuhhaupt*, Helsinki, 1955).

THE DANCE IN HRUNI CHURCH

Once, long ago, there was a priest at Hruni in Arnesysla who was very fond of merrymaking and pleasure. When people came to the church on Christmas Eve, it was always his custom to hold no service during the first part of the night, but rather to hold a great dance inside the church with his parishioners, with drinking and gambling and other unseemly sports going on far into the night. This priest had an old mother called Una; her son's ways were not at all to her liking, and she often found fault with him over them. But he paid no attention, and for many years he kept to the customs he had adopted.

One Christmas Eve the priest went on with the dancing and fun longer than usual; then his mother, who had the second sight and the gift of prophecy, went out to the church and told her son to stop the fun and start saying Mass.

But the priest says there is still ample time for that, and says: 'One more round-dance, Mother!'

So his mother went back from the church to her house. Three times over the same thing happens – Una goes out to her son and tells him to take heed of God, and to stop while things are as they are, and no worse. But he always answers in the same words as at first. But as she is walking through the church and about to leave her son for the third time, she hears someone speaking a rhyme, and catches the words:

> *Loud the mirth at Hruni,*
> *Lads sport beneath the moon-o;*
> *They'll dance to such a tune-o*
> *Men won't forget it soon-o.*
> *There'll be none left but Una,*
> *There'll be none left but Una.*

As soon as Una gets outside the church, she sees a man standing outside the door; she did not know him by sight, but she disliked the look of him, and felt sure it was he who had spoken the rhyme. She was most upset by the whole affair, and thought she could see how things were now taking a dangerous turn, for this might well be the Devil himself.

So then she takes her son's best horse and rides off in great haste to the nearest priest, and begs him to come and try to help them in their trouble, and to save her son from danger he is in. This priest goes with her at once, bringing many men with him, for the people who had been hearing Mass at his church had not yet left. But by the time they reached Hruni, the church and churchyard had sunk down into the earth, with all the people inside it, and they heard shrieking and howling from deep down underground.

One can still see traces showing that a building once stood on the high ground at Hruni, and the name is still given to a hill there and to the farm at its foot. But the story goes that after this, the site of the church was moved further down the valley to where it is now, and moreover it is said that there was never again any dancing on Christmas Eve in Hruni Church.

J.Á. II 7–8, from the Revd Jón Jónsson Nor>mann (d.1877) and the Revd Jóhann Briem (d.1894). An almost identical story is told to account for the deserted site of Bakkasta>ir in Jökuldalur (J.Á. II 6–7). At Hruni, a hollow in the earth which resembles the ground-plan of a church is pointed out as proof of the tale. As attached to that site, the story is widely known, and is told with several slight variations in the verse; it is first found mentioned in the *Dictionary* of Jón Ólafsson of Grunnavík (1705–1779), who thought that it dated from before the Reformation.

The Swedish version of this legend (ML 3070), called 'The Dance at Hårga', does not end with a building sinking but with a long line of dancers being led out by the Devil and up to a mountain top, where 'they danced till only their skulls were left' (Lindow, 148–50; Kvideland and Sehmsdorf, 294). Both the Icelandic and the Swedish tale are developments from a legend widespread in medieval Europe about sinful dancers who find themselves unable to stop. Its earliest form is 'The Dancers of Kolbeck', recorded by the monk Lambert of Hersfeld in 1075 and referring to events which supposedly occurred in 1012. It tells of a group of people who profaned a churchyard by dancing in it, and were doomed to continue without stopping for a year, and then to do penance by living as dancing beggars; in some versions they do not escape, but gradually sink down into the ground as they dance (Ward, I 196–7, 388–9).

The idea of a church sinking into the ground occurs in several other Icelandic tales where the Devil, or an evil ghost or wizard, almost brings about this calamity (cf. 'The Ghost's Son', pp.150–3 above, and J.Á. I 585, II 5–6).

'My Jon's Soul'

There were once an old cottager and his wife who lived together. The old man was rather quarrelsome and disagreeable, and, what's more, he was lazy and useless about the house; his old woman was not at all pleased about it, and she would often grumble at him and say the only thing he was any good at was squandering what she had scraped together – for she herself was constantly at work and tried by hook or by crook to earn what they needed, and was always good at getting her own way with anybody she had to deal with. But even if they did not agree about some things, the old woman loved her husband dearly and never let him go short.

Now things went on the same way for a long time, but one day the old man fell sick, and it was obvious that he was in a bad way. The old woman was sitting up with him, and when he grew weaker, it occurred to her that he could hardly be very well prepared for death, and that this meant there was some doubt as to whether he would be allowed to enter Heaven. So she thinks to herself that the best plan will be for her to try and put her husband's soul on the right road herself. Then she took a small bag and held it over her husband's nose and mouth, so that when the breath of life leaves him it passes into this bag, and she ties it up at once.

Then off she goes towards Heaven, carrying the bag in her apron, comes to the borders of the Kingdom of Heaven, and knocks on the door.

Out comes Saint Peter, and asks what her business may be.

'A very good morning to you, sir,' says the old woman. 'I've come here with the soul of that Jon of mine – you'll have heard tell of him, most likely – and now I'm wanting to ask you to let him in.'

'Yes, yes, yes,' says Peter, 'but unfortunately I can't. I have indeed heard tell of that Jon of yours, but I never heard good of him yet.'

Then the old woman said: 'Well, really, Saint Peter, I'd never have believed it, that you could be so hard-hearted! You must be forgetting what happened to you in the old days, when you denied your Master.'

At that, Peter went back in and shut the door, and the old woman remained outside, sighing bitterly. But when a little time has passed, she knocks on the door again, and out comes Saint Paul. She greets him and asks him his name, and he tells her who he is. Then she pleads with him for the soul of her Jon – but he said he didn't want to hear another word from her about that, and said that her Jon deserved no mercy.

Then the old woman got angry, and said: 'It's all very well for you, Paul! I suppose you deserved mercy in the old days, when you were persecuting God and men! I reckon I'd better stop asking any favours from you.'

So now Paul shuts the door as fast as he can. But when the old woman knocks for the third time, out comes the Blessed Virgin Mary.

'Hail, most blessed Lady,' says the old woman. 'I do hope you'll allow that Jon of mine in, even though that Peter and Paul won't allow it.'

'It's a great pity, my dear,' says Mary, 'but I daren't, because he really was such a brute, that Jon of yours.'

'Well, I can't blame you for that,' says the old woman. 'But all the same, I did think you would know that other people can have their little weaknesses as well as you – or have you forgotten by now that you once had a baby, and no father for it?'

Mary would hear no more, but shut the door as fast as she could.

For the fourth time, the old woman knocks on the door. Then out comes Christ himself, and asks what she's doing there.

Then she spoke very humbly: 'I wanted to beg you, my dear Saviour, to let this poor wretch's soul warm itself near the door.'

'It's that Jon,' answered Christ. 'No, woman; he had no faith in Me'.

Just as He said this He was about to shut the door, but the old woman was not slow, far from it – she flung the bag with the soul in it right past him, so that it hurtled far into the halls of Heaven, but then the door was slammed and bolted.

Then a great weight was lifted from the old woman's heart when Jon got into the Kingdom of Heaven in spite of everything, and she went home happy; and we know nothing more about her, nor about what became of Jon's soul after that.

J.Á. II 39–40; from the Revd Matthías Jochumsson (d.1920). There are similar jokes in medieval French and German literature about a farmer arguing at the Gates of Heaven with SS Peter, Paul and Thomas, and reminding them of their sins. The Icelandic tale seems unique in making the Virgin Mary one of the victims (Rittershaus, 343–4). The final motif in this tale causes Sveinsson to classify it as AT 330, 'The Smith Outwits the Devil', since in the latter the cunning smith sometimes gets into Heaven by hurling his magic knapsack through the gate and then wishing himself into it. There is, however, no resemblance between the rest of AT 330 and the present story, which belongs with a numerous cycle of jokes about old men and women very popular in Iceland.

BIBLIOGRAPHY AND ABBREVIATIONS

AT   *see* Aarne, A., and Thompson, S., 1961
FFC   Folklore Fellows Communications
JA   *see* Árnason, Jón, 1862–4
ML   *see* Christiansen, R. Th., 1958
Motif   *see* Thompson, S., 1955–8

Aarne, A., and Thompson, S., 1961, *The Types of the Folktale*, Helsinki (FFC 184)
A>alsteinsson, Jón Hnefill, 'Wrestling with a Ghost in Icelandic Popular Belief', *Arv* 43 (1988), 7–20
A>alsteinsson, Jón Hnefill, 'Folk Narrative and Icelandic Mythology', *Arv* 46 (1990), 115–122
A>alsteinsson, Jón Hnefill, 'The Testimony of Waking Consciousness and Dreams in Migratory Legends Concerning Human Encounters with the Hidden People', *Arv* 49 (1993), 123–131
A>alsteinsson, Jón Hnefill, 'Sæmundur fró>i: A Medieval Master of Magic', *Arv* 50 (1994), 117–132
A>alsteinsson, Jón Hnefill, 'Six Icelandic Magicians after the Time of Sæmundur fró>i', *Arv* 52 (1996), 49–62
Almquist, Bo, 'Waterhorse Legends', *Béaloideas* 59 (1991), 107–20
Almquist, Bo, 'Norwegian Dead-Child Traditions Westward Bound', in *Viking Ale*, ed. Éilís Ní Dhuibhne-Almquist and Seámas Ó Catháin (Aberystwyth, 1991), 155–67
Árnason, Jón 1863–4, *Íslenzkar fijó>sögur og Aefintýri*, Leipzig
Árnason, Jón, and Daví>sson, Ólafur, 1887–1903, *Íslenzkar Gátur, Skemmtanir, Vikivakar og fiulur*, Reykjavík
Árnason, Jón, 1954–61, *Íslenzkar fijó>sögur og Aevintýri* (3d ed., enlarged; 6 vols), Reykjavík

Ballard, Linda May, 'Before Death and Beyond', in *The Folklore of Ghosts,* ed. H.R.E. Davidson and W.M.S. Russell, 1981, 34–6

Benedikz, B.S., 1964, 'The Master Magician in Icelandic Folk-Legend', *Durham University Journal,* Dec. 1964, 22–34

Briggs, K.M., 1962, *Pale Hecate's Team,* London

Briggs, K.M., 1967, *The Fairies in Literature and Tradition,* London

Briggs, K.M., 1970, *A Dictionary of British Folk Tales in the English Language: Part A, Folk Narratives,* London

Briggs, K.M., 1971, *A Dictionary... Part B, Folk Legends,* London

Briggs, K.M., 1978, *The Vanishing People,* London

Chesnutt, Michael, 'Nordic Variants of the Guntram Legend', *Arv* 47 (1991), 153–65

Chesnutt, Michael, 'The Three Laughs', in Patricia Lysaght, Séamas Ó Catháin, and Dáthi Ó hÓgáin (eds), *Islanders and Water-Dwellers* (Dublin, 1999), 37–49

Christiansen, R.Th., 1946, 'The Dead and the Living', *Studia Norwegica* II, Oslo, 1–96

Christiansen, R.Th., 1958, *The Migratory Legends: A Proposed List of Types with a Systematic Catalogue of the Norwegian Variants,* Helsinki (FFC 175)

Christiansen, R.Th., 1959, *Studies in Irish and Scandinavian Folktales,* Copenhagen

Christansen, R.Th., 1964, *Folktales of Norway,* London

Christiansen, R.Th., and O'Suilleabhain, S., 1963, *The Types of the Irish Folktale,* Helsinki (FFC 188)

Craigie, W., 1896, *Scandinavian Folklore,* London

Davi>sson, Ólafur, 1940–3, *Galdur og Galdramál a Íslandi,* Reykjavík

Eiríksson, Hallfre>ur Örn, 'Some Icelandic Ghost Fabulates', *Arv* 49 (1993), 117–22

Erlingsson, Daví>, '*Ormur, Marmennil, Nykur:* Three Creatures of the Watery World', in Patricia Lysaght, Séamas Ó Catháin, and Dáthi Ó hÓgáin (eds), *Islanders and Water-Dwellers* (Dublin, 1999), 61–80

Gunnell, Terry, 1995, *The Origins of Drama in Scandinavia,* Cambridge

Gunnell, Terry, 'Mists, Magicians and Murderous Children: International Migratory Legends Concerning the "Black Death" in Iceland', *Northern Lights* (ed. Seámas Ó Catháin, Dublin, 2001), 47–59

Gunnell, Terry, 'The Coming of the Christmas Visitors', forthcoming in *Northern Studies*

Hafstein, Valdimar, 'The Elves' Point of View: Cultural Identity in Contemporary Icelandic Elf Tradition', *Fabula* 41:1/2 (2000), 87–104

Hartland, E.S., 1891, *The Science of Fairy Tales,* London

Hartmann, E., 1936, *Die Trollvorstellungen in den Sagen und Märchen der Skandinavischen Völker,* Stuttgart-Berlin

Kvideland, Reimund, and Henning K. Sehmsdorf, 1988, *Scandianvian Folk Belief and Legend,* Minneapolis and Oxford

Lid, N. (ed.), 1935, *Folketru. Nordisk Kultur* XIX, Stockholm-Copenhagen-Oslo

Lindow, John, 1978, *Swedish Legends and Folktales,* Berkeley and London

MacDonald, Donald Archie, 'Migratory Legends of the Supernatural in Scotland: A General Survey', in Pádraig Ó Héalaí (ed.), *Glórtha ón Osnádúr: Sounds from the Supernatural* (=*Béaloideas* 62–3, Dublin 1995), 29–78

Maurer K., 1860, *Isländische Volkssagen der Gegentvart*, Leipzig

O'Sullivan, S., 1966, *Folktales of Ireland*, London

Pentikäinen, J., 1968, *The Nordic Dead-Child Tradition*, Helsinki (FFC 202)

Powell, G.E.J., and Magnússon, Eiríkur, 1864, *Icelandic Legends* I, London

Rittershaus, A., 1902, *Die Neuisländischen Volksmärchen*, Halle

Sigfússon, Sigfús, *Íslenszkar fjó>sögur og sagnir* (11 vols., Reykjavík, 1982–93)

Simpson, Jacqueline, 1965, *The Northmen Talk*, London

Simpson, Jacqueline, 1975, *Legends of Icelandic Magicians,* Cambridge and Totowa N.J.

Simpson, Jacqueline, 1988, *Scandinavian Folktales,* London

Simpson, Jacqueline, 'Confrontational Ghost-Laying in England and Denmark' in *Northern Lights*, ed. Séamas Ó Catháin (Dublin, 2001), 305–15

Sveinsson, Einar Ól., 1929, *Verzeichnis Isländischer Märchen-varienten*, Helsinki (FFC 83)

Sveinsson, Einar Ól., 1940, *Um Íslenzkar fjó>sögur*, Reykjavik

Sveinsson, Einar Ól., 2003, *The Folk-Stories of Iceland*, transl. Benedikt Benedikz, London

Swire, O.F., 1961, *Skye: the Island and its Legends*

Sydow, C. W. von (ed.), 1931, *Folksäger och Folksagor. Nordisk Kultur* IXB, Stockholm-Copenhagen-Oslo

Tangherlini, T.R., 'Ships, Fogs, and Travelling Pairs: Plague Legend Migration in Scandinavia', *Journal of American Folklore* 400 (1988), 176–206

Thomas, K., 1971, *Religion and the Decline of Magic*, London

Thompson, S., 1955–8, *Motif-Index of Folk-Literature*, Copenhagen and Bloomington, Indiana

Thomson, D., 1965, *The People of the Sea* (2nd ed.), London

Thorpe, Benjamin, 1851/2001, *Northern Mythology*, London/Ware

Tubach, F. C., 1969, *Index Exemplorum*, Helsinki (FFC 204)

Ward, Donald (ed. and transl.), 1981, *The German Legends of the Brothers Grimm*, London

West, John F., 1980, *Faroese Folktales and Legends,* Lerwick

Westwood, Jennifer, 1985, *Albion*, London

Wildhaber, R., 1955, *Das Sündenregister auf der Kuhhaupt*, Helsinki (FFC 163)

Williamson, K., 1970, *The Atlantic Islands* (2nd ed.), London

INDEX OF TALE TYPES

Numbers preceded by AT are from Antti Aarne and Stith Thompson, *The Types of the Folktale* 1961; those with ML are from R. Th. Christiansen, *The Migratory Legends* 1958; those with ML and an asterisk are from K.M. Briggs, *A Dictionary of British Folktales*, 1970–1.

Bracketed numbers indicate that the resemblance between the international tale and the Icelandic tale is only partial.

GENERAL INDEX